The
New
Historicism

The
New
Historicism

Gina Hens-Piazza

FORTRESS PRESS
Minneapolis

THE NEW HISTORICISM

0-8006-2989-2

The paper used in this publication meets the minimum requirements of American National Standard for Information Sciences—Permanence of Paper for Printed Library Materials, ANSI Z329.48-1984.

Manufactured in the U.S.A.   AF 1-2989

07   06   05   04   03   02   1   2   3   4   5   6   7   8   9   10

For Hannah

Contents

Acknowledgments

In my experience, writing is always a communal endeavor. This project is no exception. In many ways, the persistent conversations and questions of my students and colleagues around this topic over the past few years make me more a scribe for collective consciousness than anything bespeaking an author. While I bear full responsibility for the final outcome here, many who will remain unnamed have contributed to the production of this work. Colleagues and students at the Graduate Theological Union, the University of California, Berkeley, the University of Wisconsin, Stephens Point, and my own school, the Jesuit School of Theology at Berkeley number among those contributors.

In particular, my sincere appreciation goes to my friend and colleague, John Donahue, S.J., for both his sustained interest in the topic and his encouragement to "get it down." Sandra Schneiders, I.H.M., my cherished friend and colleague at the Jesuit School of Theology, remained my persistent interrogator and critic along the way. Harold Washington, with whom I currently co-chair a session on New Historicism and the Hebrew Bible in the Society of Biblical Literature, read and provided invaluable comments near the completion of the project. I am deeply grateful for his time and careful work. Most especially, I am indebted to Ann Naffziger and Bula Maddison for their tireless editing at every stage of writing. Were I to reference their contributions, every page would bear their names.

Finally, my family continues to be the persistent support and the mainstay in all my projects. To Fred, in particular, I can only continue to say thanks. His interest and encouragement remain constant and boundless.

1
Introduction

Many years ago, poet Geoffrey Chaucer observed that folks long to go on pilgrimages. This study results from a pilgrimage of sorts. It began on the East Coast and ended on the West Coast. I had accepted an academic appointment to teach Old Testament at the Jesuit School of Theology at the Graduate Theological Union some years ago and needed to do something to emancipate myself from my New York City identity and prepare for my new academic home in Berkeley. So during my cross-country sojourn, I began reading the New Historicists, a group of literary critics associated with the University of California at Berkeley. But there was more to my scheme than mere desire to adapt to my new professional environs.

Over the past century, biblical studies has hosted an array of methodological approaches.[1] The succession tale of this methodological parade is a familiar one. Up until thirty years ago, historical studies held sway in the biblical field where the factors external to the text were considered integral in production of meaning. Authorial intention, context, sources, editorial process, and literary form constituted the locus of study. Methods developed that systematically analyzed these factors in the service of interpretation. Many of these approaches are still practiced today. Form critics classify individual literary units and search for their probable "setting in life."[2] Tradition critics study the origins, composition, and transmission of the biblical writings. Social science critics study the cultural matrix extrinsic to the texts. Redaction critics detail the theological interests and intentions of the compilers.

Under the aegis of historical critical studies, specialization has continued to grow while reaping important gains. Biblical studies has been liberated from parochialism. Study of the biblical text is now a respected and

1

funded enterprise within the public sector. Biblical scholars regularly collaborate with colleagues in other areas of the humanities. These exchanges across academic disciplines have been especially apparent and productive in literary studies of the Bible.

In recent years this appropriation of methods from schools of literary criticism has created what some have called a "paradigm shift" and what others have labeled as a "revolution" in the biblical field. Instead of referring to the Bible as Scripture as was common in historical studies, the Bible is spoken about as literature. Meaning once tied to text in relation to context is now often consigned to the text alone. Analysis of the biblical stories for literary coherence, rhetorical elements, narrative design, deep structures, poetics, and all other kinds of literary pursuits have challenged the sovereignty and reign of the historical critical inquiry. Mark Powell's anthology of modern literary studies on the Bible attests to the burgeoning status of the field.[3] Cataloging research during the past twenty years, Powell lists well over 1,000 studies on biblical texts that employ literary methods. These studies are matched in number by other explorations that discuss the theoretics of literary approaches to the Bible by biblical scholars and literary critics alike.

Evidence of this shift is not confined to the kinds of research being produced. Changes in the curricula of degree programs in biblical studies bears witness. Students in pursuit of doctoral degrees across the country often bypass historical study of the traditions and, instead, are being trained in literary theory and approaches. The work and identity of many scholars themselves tends to be yoked less with areas of the biblical canon and more with the literary approaches they employ.

This shift in the biblical field away from historical studies and toward the full-scale embrace of literary approaches makes a group of literary critics called New Historicists especially strange if not intriguing. Given the direction of the development of approaches during this century, is a literary approach called "New Historicism" not a contradiction in terms? Still, as I began my reading, I wondered if New Historicism might be a means to cross over the sharply drawn border that currently separates historical studies from literary studies in the biblical field. Thus began my journey. My pilgrimage from East to West marked the beginning of a sojourn in a vast academic terrain where a rendezvous with the New Historicists proved frustrating as well as exhilarating.

It was frustrating because no one as yet has offered an operational definition that domesticates this literary novum for straightforward public consumption. Stephen Greenblatt refers to New Historicism as "a trajectory" rather than a set of beliefs.[4] Louis Montrose calls it an "orientation" rather than a prescription of practices.[5] Joel Fineman defines it as an "intellectual posture."[6] And Catherine Gallagher describes it as a "phenomenon of apparent political indeterminacy."[7] Moreover, since New Historicist readings initially focused upon Renaissance literature, I have even gone back and read some of those Shakespearean plays I was supposed to read in high school and college in order to get a handle on what this new breed of critic is up to. But the theoretical explanation and methodological specification I went after is not what I found. Instead, I discovered an academic landscape of criticism that accommodates an eclectic array of studies. Murdering peasants as an art form, England as the only all-transvestite theater, rock and roll and the art of soldiering in Indochina, and the human ear in Shakespeare's sonnets number among New Historicism's investigations.

Further, the variety that prevails in content also persists in practice. Some studies use a literary text to map power relations in a society. Some reconstruct discourse by examining extraneous cultural artifacts. Some make comparisons between a play and a pamphlet, a novel and medical literature, a letter and a cant term. Others focus upon the contradictions, tensions, and aporia in writings. To make matters worse, New Historicists are not only heterogeneous in their practices but are characteristically reticent to theorize about their strategies.[8] Fineman describes New Historicism's distinctiveness specifically as "its programmatic refusal to specify a methodological program for itself—its characteristic air of reporting, haplessly, the discoveries it happened serendipitously to stumble upon in the course of undirected, idle rambles through the historical archives."[9] I had hoped to uncover a blueprint joining historical and literary concerns that I could use for my own work on biblical texts. But to my consternation and dismay, I have been unsuccessful in my attempts to map a method here.

Strangely, this experience of exasperation has become at the same time an experience of exhilaration. Several years ago, while defending my dissertation, I had a close-to-fatal mishap. The project was a method study in which I set forth a sociorhetorical approach whereby the literary and social worlds of texts were brought together in interpretation. Not surprisingly, all this research and writing about "method" and about connections between texts and contexts made me increasingly aware of the inherent fallacies in what I was proposing. So, in the conclusion of the study, I set forth my observation that "method appeared to be more like a codification of our hunches about texts" and that "interpretations that separate texts and contexts do so primarily in the service of our own methodological machinations."[10] Little did I know that I had taken on the very foundation of methodological specialization that had held sway for most of this century in biblical studies. This passing observation in the conclusion of my study became a major point of contestation during the defense and subsequently an occasion for a "minor" but necessary revision. I conceded my error, made the correction, and received my diploma, only to have my "ignorance" rekindled when I began reading the New Historicists.

New Historicists are often charged by their critics with "anecdote spinning," the kind which I have just indulged in. It is true and perhaps strange that anecdotes are common and crucial to any practice identified as a "historicism." Normally, we do not tend to think of anecdote when we think of history. In fact, we are trained to think the opposite. Unlike historical assessments that strive to be general and universal, the identification "anecdote" derives from its particular and individual character. It is often personal and partisan. It derails the serious progression of history with a playful pause. It disrupts the successivity of history and interrupts its logic. Indeed, works that succumb to such features risk the negative assessment of their historical value as "anecdotal."

By contrast, New Historicists claim anecdote as foundational to their work. Joel Fineman's definition of anecdote as "a historeme, . . . the smallest minimal unit of the historiographic fact" suggests its integral function to doing history as distinguished from past ways of proceeding.[11] First, anecdote resists location in the teleological continuum of beginning—middle—end we construct in organizing the past. At the same time, it escapes the historical positivist explanations of cause and effect we employ to construe historical progression. Instead, anecdote just lets history happen.

Anecdotes are crucial among New Historicists because they transport a key feature of history, namely contingency—but contingency in all its fullness. Contingency, as a central concept, functions to expose both the conditional as well as the accidental as the dynamic of historical unfoldings.

Contingency refers to that which may or may not happen as well as that which predictably occurs due to a precondition. Moreover, a history founded upon the fullness of contingency puts it into practice. It accommodates all the accidentals, the arbitrariness, the wanderings, the coincidences of experience. My move from New York City to the Berkeley area and the brush with academic misfortune while defending my dissertation together make up the "the accidentals" that haplessly coincided as prelude to this study. At the same time, these coincidences reside alongside the conditions that explain my interest in this project at this particular time. Drawing upon causal logic, my anecdote structures how everything is conditional or dependent upon everything else. My being in Berkeley at this time, my education at this particular juncture in biblical studies, and the close-to-fatal mishap during the defense of my dissertation serve as the conditions that logically explain my interest and initiative for this project. Effortlessly, anecdote exposes the fullness of contingency, that is, its capacity to accommodate both the accidental and conditional in the construction of the past and in the historical writing about it. New Historicism as a literary-critical movement is governed by such interests. Subject to its own assumptions about how the past is constructed, an air of contingency accompanies even the labeling of this practice.

While the term New Historicism can be traced to an essay by Michael McCanles in 1980,[12] Stephen Greenblatt, the *chef d'école* of the program, claims to have coined the label somewhat arbitrarily.[13] Earlier, in his *Renaissance Self-Fashioning,* which is generally taken as the programmatic work in this area, Greenblatt describes his way of working as a "poetics of culture."[14] Others working in this area have other labels. "The new history," "historical-materialist criticism," "cultural materialism," and "critical historicism" are among the candidates.[15] Because of a general reticence about theoretical or methodological identification, some have rejected labels altogether. Lee Patterson, a practitioner of this orientation, has observed that "no single label can be usefully applied to the historicist enterprise as a school, least of all the already assigned, hotly contested, and irredeemably vague 'New Historicism.'"[16] Despite the debate as to what to call it, as well as the motley conglomeration of its concerns and practices, some preliminary observations serve as introduction to a discussion of this innovation in literary studies.

New Historicism arose as a literary-critical movement at the University of California at Berkeley in the 1980s and quickly spread to other American universities. While it does not disregard the findings of past literary history, where and how New Historicism digresses from these earlier forms of criticism shapes its contours.

At the start, it should be noted that New Historicism is less a theory and certainly not a method. Adopting Daniel Boyarin's suggestion, New Historicism will be discussed here as a sensibility or perspective on literature.[17] As perspective, it views texts in materialistic terms, a position it shares with cultural materialism.[18] Texts are caught up in the social processes and contexts out of which they emerge. Though identified with a single author, texts are generated by a community. This community produces a text while another community reads it and thus are its consumers. Hence, New Historicism trains its view upon the processes of production and consumption of texts.

Since New Historicism will be talked about here as sensibility rather than as method, a more fitting starting point might be to describe the assumptions that fashion such a mind-set instead of describing what it does. Four assumptions serve to craft the description:

1. Literature is viewed as integrally tied to and identified with other material realities that make up a social context.

2. Viewing literature as on par with other types of texts, the privileging of literature or its composition over and above other social practices is rejected.

3. Characteristic distinctions between literature and history are sidelined.

4. The constructions of the past are presumed as intimately tied to the present.

First, New Historicism views literature like other social and cultural practices, artifacts, relics, and data of a context. Like displays we might see in a gallery or museum, texts stand alongside other cultural "texts." Together with other remnants, relics, and vestiges of the past, they craft a social context anthropologically. Of interest here is how, not what, forces (historical, social, economic, biographical, sexual, aesthetic, psychological, and so on) interact with these productions and interpretive practices. In the course of such inquiries, New Historicism crosses disciplinary boundaries venturing into the territories of economics, medicine, psychology, and law, to name only a few.

6

Second, this repositioning of literature in relation to other sociocultural materials levels the playing field in terms of reigning distinctions. The privileging of literature or its composition over and above other social practices or remnants of the past is rejected. Literature is on equal footing with all other "cultural texts." Literature as "high culture" has no priority or elevated status over other elements that attract the label "popular culture." These very distinctions, high culture and popular culture, are cultural practices themselves warranting examination. Together, literature — along with other cultural vestiges—contributes to the construction we call context and to the story we call history.

Third, the enlistment of literary texts along with other cultural phenomena in the makeup of context necessitates a redefinition of literature in relation to social context and social history. Distinctions such as foreground/background, superstructure/substructure, cultural reality/mirror image are no longer accurate or adequate delineations by which to understand literature in relation to other social or historical contexts. Instead, literature and social context are thought to reside in a dynamic relationship of mutual shaping and defining of one another. How literature influences the construction of social context and how social context impacts the production of literature defines New Historicism's interests. Hence, New Historicism views the relationship between literature and other cultural phenomena as reciprocal and mutually productive. Negotiations and exchanges take place in each of their constructions.

Finally, New Historicists recognize that these relationships and transactions are not confined to the past but are shaped by the values and experience of those in the present studying the past. Thus, New Historicism resists hard and fast distinctions that separate now/then, author/reader, what the text meant/what the text means, and even composition/interpretation. All these long-held categories that reinforce distinctions between past and present begin to erode in the New Historicist's view.

Now if all this sounds a little unwieldy, take heart. On the heels of this first chapter, the following discussion will attempt to map the contours of this New Historicism with description, contrasts, illustrations, and inquiry. Chapter 2 offers an overview of those thinkers and their works that have contributed to this new way of proceeding in literary studies. Chapter 3 seeks to clarify New Historicism in relation to and in contrast to the assumptions and concerns of "old" historicism or historicism as we've known it. In chapter 4, the features that recur across New Historicist studies are set forth and discussed. Illustrations of these features, as well as the different types of studies that occur under the rubric "New Historicism," serve to focus chapter 5. Finally, chapter 6 discusses New Historicism's contributions and shortcomings along with the questions it raises in biblical studies.

As we travel across this terrain, there may be times when it seems we are without a compass or we lack the kind of surefootedness to which we have been accustomed. The well-defined distinctions between text and context, history and literature, past and present begin to disappear in a New Historicist's inquiry. The well-circumscribed entities—authorial intention, literary unity, audience response, organizing theme—that we have learned to count on in biblical studies fade as foci in this kind of work. In place of all these outcomes emerges a more fragmentary view of the text as well as a more fragmentary view of ourselves. In return, New Historicism seeks to offer sufficient compensatory satisfaction on the journey called biblical interpretation—namely the disclosure of the half-hidden cultural transactions in which the biblical story and we, the reader/interpreter, participate.

2
Historicizing
the New Historicism

Tracing the development of New Historicism risks contradiction. The enlistment of theory, definitions, frameworks, and chronology to sketch a description too readily conforms to the insular, one-dimensional, monologic portraits of the past that New Historicists themselves decry. In the end, an account of the influences and developments of New Historicism may be less a reflection of the multiple, complex, and interacting elements that make up New Historicism's past and more a reflection of a desire to harness this movement so as to claim understanding.

In order to practice the self-consciousness that so characterizes New Historicist projects, this effort acknowledges these risks as well as the partisan character of what follows. It sets forth one history of the many stories that could be told about the rise of this movement. It attempts to craft a story of the past by tracing filiations between various theorists' work and New Historicism. It attends to the years immediately preceding its identification on the campus at the University of California at Berkeley, and it identifies the thinking and works of key figures or groups that appear as a prelude to New Historicism's recognition and productions. Moreover, because New Historicist projects are themselves cultural artifacts, it considers briefly the possible symbiotic relationship between the politics of our society and the appearance of New Historicism at this time. Motivating this organization and narrative of New Historicism's past is a desire to make a case and an appeal for a New Historicism in biblical studies in the present. The discussion concludes, therefore, by forging links between the literary, methodological, and institutional questions New Historicism raises and related issues currently discussed in the biblical field.

THEORETICAL TENDENCIES

The heterogeneous character of New Historicism is often explained in light of its theoretical reticence or even evasiveness. True, no one critical theory can begin to garner unanimous approval as the foundation of New Historicism or even serve as the common thread that binds together the eclectic array of practices and the various kinds of studies conducted under this aegis. Yet a traceable resonance of influences and confluences echoes consistently enough across these various projects to merit some citation.

First, in varying degrees, many New Historicist studies manifest a theoretical kinship with Marx and, to a more significant degree, with Foucault. While not all New Historicists acknowledge Marxist influence (some even deny it), the key concepts are prevalent enough to incite Edward Pechter's pejorative labeling of the enterprise as "Marxist criticism."[1] The frequent focus upon struggle, contestation, and power relations in New Historicist studies invites such labeling. If New Historicism owes a theoretical debt to Marx, however, it stems primarily from his development of a theory of ideology.[2] Ideology narrates a class consciousness invented to represent its world. Always arbitrary, the consciousness is developed and sustained by a culture's habits of symbol making. Ideology then is cultural and always contingent upon dominant class needs. Etched in the institutions, customs, writings, and mores of a society, ideology invites the kind of study that can discern and critique its construction.

While issues stemming from ideology critique occupy the New Historicists, they are less comfortable working within the social sciences in any formal sense. Offering a social scientist's critique of ideology or considering such matters as the superstructure and base of imputed class consciousness is outside their immediate training and purview as literary critics. Though deeply committed and attendant to the social and political forces at work in the structuring of a society, they are more suited to search for such traces by studying representations in texts. Hence, though interested in Marxist theory, New Historicists have moved in the direction of redefining "the notion of ideology critique into discourse analysis."[3] As a practice, discourse analysis scrutinizes texts for how they serve the interests of class relations or appraises texts for how they participate in the discourse of power relations.

Following Foucault's influential usage, literature as discourse "emphasizes literature as a process rather than simply a set of products; a process which is intrinsically social, connected at every point with mechanisms and the institutions that mediate and control the flow of knowledge and power in a community."[4] Among poststructuralists, the writings of Michel Foucault have enjoyed a most enthusiastic reception within the humanities and especially among literary critics.[5] If an identifiable theoretical base could be established for the tenacious resistance to theory among New Historicists, it would most certainly be the work of Foucault. A reluctant theorist himself, Foucault refused identification with or elaboration of any univocal concepts in his work. Systematic theory itself takes part in a logic of representation that for Foucault only encourages erroneous assumptions. He rejects the notion of a subject who stands outside any conceptual representation, and he argues against the transparency of language which assumes words can represent things. Transgressing the limits that such assumptions would impose, Foucault offers two key notions for our discussions, that of history and of texts.

First, in considering history, Foucault rejects the linear model of history as an unearned form of metaphysical self-assurance.[6] He refrains from historical language that is totalizing, contiguous, or teleological. Every period is more complicated than the paradigm that ordered it. There are no historical local totalities where everybody thinks the same, acts the same, or lives in the same manner. In rejecting a history that is rational and seeking an explanation for an event in terms of one-dimensional economic or political forces, he opts for a more complicated view of history. History is made up of numerous discourses—medical, economic, biological, and so on—each with its own characteristics and duration. His own writings reflect this complexity and resist identification with any one discipline. The scope of his work includes books on sexuality, illness, madness, economics, crime and punishment, and the role of power in discourse. Hayden White aptly characterizes Foucault's writing: "It looks like history, like philosophy, like criticism, but it stands over against these discourses as ironic antithesis."[7]

Second, Foucault views texts within very broad, unbridled categories—as part of a larger framework of texts, customs, practices, and institutions. This enlarged notion of text complicates interpretation. It attends to the many connections between a given text and other texts—cultural texts, material contexts, and intellectual contexts—and thus invites intertextual readings and interpretations.

11

Aware of the shaping power of discursive activity, Foucault looks to texts for signs of their social and political impact as well as for imprints of the social and political forces upon the text. Amidst these connections, texts are studied for articulated hierarchies of value, power, and meaning. Any powerful institution necessarily controls the very meaning of discourse used to discuss it. As he explores the relationship between power and language, between discourse and politics, he seeks to hear the voices excluded from history. His search for traces of those who remained unassimilated into the narratives of power is said to have always been a prime focus of his studies. However, by power, Foucault does not necessarily mean force or negative coercion. He says power "doesn't weigh on us as a force that says no, but that it traverses and produces things, it induces pleasure, forms of knowledge, produces discourse. It needs to be considered as a productive network which runs through the whole social body, much more than as a negative instance whose function is repression."[8] Hence, Foucault urges pursuit of human history through a study of discourse and power.

Nowhere has the relation between discourse and power been more persuasively and disturbingly illustrated than in the recent work of feminists, ethnic minorities, and Third World critics.[9] The insights and assumptions of these scholars have both shaped and motivated the critical practice of New Historicism. Collectively, their work has raised some of the most significant questions in historical studies about how the past is recorded, and in literary studies about the so-called objective results of text-centered interpretations claimed by formalists and essentialists. Feminist criticism in particular has actually served as a "model for new historicism in that it has inspired its adherents to identify new objects for study, bring those objects into the light of critical attention, and insist upon their legitimate place in the curriculum."[10]

Women's studies in the academy has unsettled aesthetic hierarchies that have limited or manipulated our view of the significance of women in culture. Their narratives of their own experience in society and in the academy have revealed just how socially and politically contingent academic practices are. In addition, they have exposed the contingency of even the products of these efforts, the so-called "universal truths." Further, the production of women's histories as counterhistories have found company in and encouraged the composition of the histories of ethnic groups, racial minorities, and "the people."

Judith Newton has observed, "Feminist politics and feminist theory . . . along with black liberation movement and the new left, have helped generate the 'postmodern' assumption about the 'objectivity,' the construction of the subject, and the cultural power of representation currently identified with 'new historicism'. . . ."[11] Moreover, the kinds of studies conducted by women, ethnic and racial groups, and Third World scholars make abundantly clear the nature of the shift that is taking place. The construction of a past that characterized the Old Historicism is being supplanted and replaced by studies of how the past is constructed, the New Historicism.

This turn toward the processes by which history is produced involves a great deal of anthropological torque. In particular, the influence of cultural anthropologist Clifford Geertz and his approach to culture, "thick description," echoes resoundingly across essays by New Historicists.[12] Borrowing from Max Weber, Geertz defines cultures as "webs of significance." Literary, economic, religious, and aesthetic conventions make up these webs. Thick description strives to discover, sort out, and detail the significant features, layers, and networks of human discourse, interactions, institutions, contexts, behaviors, and conventions. It burrows deep into the labyrinth of a social world. Descriptions of its findings seek to capture the significant import and potential meaning of social reality itself.

It is Geertz's claims about what he observes that distinguish him from how anthropologists have proceeded in the past and that make his work so appealing to New Historicists in the present. What "we" anthropologists call "our data," Geertz writes, "are really our own constructions of other people's constructions of what they and their compatriots are up to."[13] This "little drama," as he refers to field notes, is as much if not more about explication than it is about observation.

In studying culture, Geertz views events or institutions as texts. He excavates and analyzes the minute particulars of these texts, be it a cockfight in Bali, sheep-stealing in Morocco, or funeral practices in Java. He likens the composition of his "little drama" or his field notes to the outcome of close readings produced by literary critics. In the process, his intensive scrutiny of these cultural texts yields a thick description that discloses the dynamics of a whole society, the lineaments of an entire culture.

New Historicists have adopted and adapted Geertz's approach. As Geertz studies culture as texts, New Historicists study texts as a culture. They focus variously upon whole texts, a stanza of a poem, letters, a court report. They analyze and interrogate it in all its particulars so as to reveal something about its parts and their roles in construing cultural reality. They study it in conjunction with other contemporaneous events, objects, and texts in such a way that "a mutual illumination occurs and a cultural paradigm is revealed."[14]

It is in the outcome, however, that New Historicists part company with Geertz. His analysis tends to produce a cohesion of cultural meaning, a unified, integral, cultural whole that is celebrated and praiseworthy as art. Instead, New Historicists are interested in the fragmentary and contested production of their texts. They search out the way that cultural meanings are related to the political and ideological domains. They try to uncover traces in texts that signal contest, struggle, and oppression. Roger Keesing's critique of Geertz details and distinguishes the concerns that shape the New Historicist enterprise. In contrast to New Historicists and their interests, Geertz's cultural descriptions are "silent on the way cultural meanings sustain power and privilege . . . blind to the political consequences of cultures as ideologies, their situatedness serve as justifications and mystifications of a local historically cumulated status quo."[15]

PRECEDENTS

In addition to the formative influence of Foucault, feminists, and Geertz, the contributions of other significant figures in the area of history, culture, and literature also echo across some of the working assumptions of New Historicist studies. In his work *Marxism and Literature,* Raymond Williams, from whom the term cultural materialism derives, sets forth a notion of culture that inspired the rehistoricization of literary studies.[16] Culture is not a fixed pattern of beliefs and meanings. Rather it is a dynamic process of representation and interpretation, an irreducibly plural social formation. In refining Marxist notions of dominant culture, he argues that no culture, even an apparently dominant hegemonic culture, is ever static, total, or exclusive. Rather, "it is being continually resisted, limited, altered, challenged by pressures not at all its own."[17] Hence, culture must be viewed as an ongoing process being "continually renewed, recreated, defended, and modified."[18] Social meanings, identities, institutions, and mores are constantly in process, undergoing negotiation and exchanges. Literature as one of the forums for these productions of social meanings and identities is itself necessarily caught up in these negotiations and exchanges with other elements in the culture. Such an understanding challenges the notion of literature as "aesthetic" creation, as something set apart from the "common" or even "popular" cultural formations.

More precisely, this dynamic understanding of the relationship between culture and literature presses the question of the relationship between the aesthetic productions and social productions, between the private and the public realm, between literature and politics, between history and context. Hayden White, in his work *Tropics of Discourse*, collapsed the idea of history and the idea of literary texts. He reduces them both to the tropological, that is, to figurative forms of speech.[19] The consequences of collapsing these distinctions are clear. Participating in these cultural negotiations and exchanges, both historical and literary texts are socially produced and socially productive.

Earlier, Mikhail Bakhtin anticipated and elaborated this view of texts in his work.[20] Literature is not monologic, expressive of a single political vision. It is polyvalent. It is composed of "unofficial" voices echoing other values, touting competing viewpoints, contesting the prevailing powers, subverting and even parodying the dominant discourse. Bakhtin's term for this multivalent property of literature is "heteroglossia."

The rejection of literature and culture as totalizing, insular, and monologic coincided with what was to become another insight resonating across the academy—the growing recognition of the exclusivity and dominance of the Eurocentric cultural discourse as representative of universal discourse. Edward Said's important work, *Orientalism*, illustrates and encourages the widespread critique of Western discourse as universal and of the preeminence of the Western literary canon.[21] Around the same time, Frank Lentricchia's publication of *After the New Criticism* links "the antihistorical impulses of formalist theories of literary criticism" with one-dimensional theories of history.[22] He dismantles the teleological and totalizing conceptions of "history" that had dominated in earlier years. He calls for the emergence of a historicism that takes stock of the "resisting forces of heterogeneity, contradiction, fragmentation, and difference."[23]

With the publication of *Renaissance Self-Fashioning*, a decidedly New Historicism arose in Renaissance studies under the aegis of Stephen Green-

15

blatt at the University of California, Berkeley.[24] In his subsequent works, Greenblatt continues to study literature in such a way as to illuminate the power relations in the courts, colonial society, church, and military administration of Renaissance culture.[25] But this emphasis on the cultural production of texts has not confined itself to Renaissance studies. The work of Jerome McGann suggests its impact upon British Romantic studies.[26] Sacvan Bercovitch and Myra Jehlen's collection *Ideology and Classic American Literature* (1986) attests to its influence in American literary studies.[27]

Louis Montrose explains the enthusiasm for New Historicism and its rapid spread across literary studies and concurrently across the humanities in cultural terms. This turn toward history needs to be understood as "a compensation for that acceleration in the forgetting of history that seems to characterize an increasingly technocratic and future-oriented academy and society."[28] At the same time, others understood the insatiable interest for a New Historicism in opposite terms. Here its rise is thought of as a "sympathetic response to the concern for history among contemporary writers and artists."[29]

New Historicists themselves cite the political conditions of the time as contributing to its development. In the 1980s, the Reagan-Bush era signaled the definitive end to the Left's thriving political influence of the 1960s and early 1970s. In response, the Left retreated to the academy where it believed it could still work on and work out its causes. Commitments in the political and social arena then translated into politically and historically aware scholarship. This ethos, often thought of as countercultural activity, assumed many forms at both the level of the institution and within individual departments. At the institutional level, it became apparent that the academy is not isolated from or disinterested in national politics. The academy, with its hiring, tenuring, and administrative policies, is often allied with centers of economic and political power. In departments such as literature and history, it provoked an evaluation of the assumed aesthetic integrity of literary works and the objective claims of historicists' strategies. Gradually, these countercultural currents in the academy made clear the social and political consequences of the way history was written and literary texts were read.

Finally, the conditions within literary criticism itself were ripe for the formalization of a New Historicism. For many, New Historicism emerges as the predictable next stage in the development of literary theory and academic writing. While some understand it as the antidote to deconstruction and its denial of context,[30] others, viewing deconstruction itself as a historicizing theory, perceive a more complementary relationship between the two.[31] In addition, New Historicism's attention to issues of power in composition, reading, and interpretation finds ready reception among those advocates of recent approaches who attend to what difference readers make. Finally, New Historicism's overarching interests in texts as cultural production make for an easy alliance with the growing prominence of cultural studies in the academy in general and within literary studies in particular. In concert with all these conditions along with others we do not even recognize or fail to relate here, New Historicism can be counted as heralding a new era, in both the predictable and accidental developments of theory and method in literary studies.

As New Historicism spreads across the academic terrain, its range of practitioners extends beyond the confines of departments of literature and includes those interested in feminist, Marxist, ethnic, and cultural studies. What joins together this loose if not aberrant confederacy of critics across the humanities is their return to history after a long exile and their lively production of a *new* historicism. Hence, its recent attraction to scholars in biblical studies may be in part an appeal for trendiness or even a nostalgia for history. At the same time, there is something urgent and legitimate about the attraction. Biblical scholars wrestle with New Historicism because of its willingness to wrestle with some of the same theoretical, methodological, and institutional issues that the biblical guild confronts at this time.

THE APPEAL OF/FOR
A NEW HISTORICISM IN BIBLICAL STUDIES

Trends in biblical studies have often appeared as a late shadow of those same moves already well established or even fading in literary studies in the academy. The recent innovations in historical approaches to the biblical history are no exception. Like the currents in literary studies, the move away from the formalistic practices of New Criticism with its view of texts as verbal icons in biblical studies was prompted by readings that transgressed formalism's well-established boundaries between text and context. Traces of sociohistorical, psychological, and linguistic structures of the ancient world are identified within the biblical traditions. At the same time, the canons of close readings and other text-centered methods have been summarily challenged by the rise of reader-oriented approaches. Today, many biblical scholars read texts from the perspective of a professed ideology (feminist, Third World, Marxist, and so on). This focus upon the dynamics of reading has necessarily evolved not only into an embrace of the individual reader but also a preoccupation with his or her history and sociocultural context. On the shoulders of such theoretical moves, the return to history in biblical studies broadens its scope. In place of text-centered studies, the focus on history includes both that of the text and that of the reader as well as the negotiations between the two. A New Historicism in biblical studies accommodates such dynamics.

Another explanation for the appeal of a New Historicism in biblical studies moves beyond the narrow confines of currents in literary studies on the Bible and focuses instead on the present state of methodological practices of the biblical guild itself. However, unlike the reasons that often justify the rise of new methods or approaches, the interest in New Historicism does not stem from the assessment of how past and current methods have failed. The yield of historical methods and the harvests of literary approaches in biblical studies have been richly successful. The array of critical social-scientific and historical approaches has produced an expansive catalogue of information about the ancient biblical world. Moreover, the rapidly growing collection of literary-critical approaches continues to illuminate the rich poetics and artistry of the biblical texts, as well as disclose their political import for readers and the readers' role in the interpretive process. But as the parameters of individual historical methods are defined and the theoretical boundaries of newer literary and cultural approaches are sketched, the gap between these two arenas widens. The possibility of ever arriving at an integrated grasp of our subject fades. Synchronic approaches undermine diachronic methods.[32] A focus on context contrasts with a focus on text.[33] Literary analysis frequently involves setting aside the research and conclusions of historical critics.[34] Different approaches to interpretation engender polarization on the determinacy or indeterminacy of meaning.[35] While such disagreements can be productive, they can also encourage fragmentation. Methodological specialization in biblical studies now threatens to be replaced by methodological ghettos.

Biblical studies has become insular. It appears as a profession of specialists, refining and defending their methods, parsing these sophisticated approaches further in the form of sub-specialties. As specialization continues to grow more intense and detailed, each sub-specialty sketches its own parameters, generates its own sets of questions, cultivates a highly distinctive vocabulary, and creates its own task forces. Ironically the biblical text as the discourse of faith communities, who publicly profess and share a common belief and look toward the day when "all will be one," has become within the biblical guild the object of highly privatized study.

New Historicism, on the other hand, abandons such specialization. It crosses boundaries separating the different disciplinary specializations and ignores the boundaries separating the world of the text and the world of the reader. It invites critics to address the political consequences, economic ramifications, social functions, and ethical import of the texts in their historical *and* in their contemporary contexts. It assumes that any social historical construction that one might compose is not only founded upon a production of the past but also results in a production about a reader. Consequently, this construction must be seen in relation to the ancient writing and contemporary reading and the ideological and institutional agendas that lie behind the writing and the reading practices.

This explicit and mutual engagement of reader and text in the historical work abandons the once hallowed but now dated distinction between "what the text meant and what a text means" in biblical studies. The subjective disposition, cultural location, and ideological bias of the reader is not only acknowledged, it moves to the foreground and is considered tantamount to meaning in every stage of the interpretation process. Hence, a new set of questions occupy the new historian in biblical studies. Whose history does criticism relate? What transactions take place in the ancient and contemporary context in history's production? How does that history get told? Who is empowered to do the telling? What changes in the social fabric does biblical studies effect—or fail to effect? In the wake of these shifts, anything approximating a one-dimensional totalizing explanation of history, context, or even of the biblical text itself is suspect.

At the same time, the long-standing distinction between the world behind the text and the world of the text is dismantled. As artifacts, the biblical texts, along with potsherds, seals, scarabs, and so on, are interwoven in the texture of culture. They commingle messily with other realities of the sociocultural terrain. They contribute to the make-up of culture, while at the same time elements of culture affect their make-up. In order to be faithful to the very nature of the biblical writings as texts, therefore, interpretation must somehow investigate concurrently the sociocultural impact of the world in the literary text and sociocultural impact to the world of the literary text.

Beyond literary currents and the current condition of methodological specialization in the biblical guild looms another explanation for the appeal of a New Historicism in biblical studies—namely, the institutional challenge of the future. Over the past fifteen to twenty years, the academic locations where biblical studies are taught—colleges, universities, theological centers, and seminaries—have experienced a sea change in the manner in which they conduct themselves as instigated under the banner of cultural diversity. This diversification has affected both faculty composition and the make-up of student population, particularly in the United States. Until recently, these institutions, analogous to modern society and its industrial model of a factory, fashioned the academic or professional religion specialists from a common raw material, that is, white, middle-class males.

Today, the dominance of the once homogenous character of these institutions has all but vanished. Women and men (and often, more women than men) from the Pacific Rim, Asia, Latin America, Africa, and the racial minorities of this country have reconstituted the administration, student bodies, and faculties of these institutions. In addition, the students and faculty of denominational seminaries as well as theological centers and university-based religion departments, represent an array of religious traditions, sexual orientations, and ages. The curriculum, pedagogy, administrative models, and financial aid packages suited for the past are undergoing major renovation and rethinking. Moreover, the disciplinary specialization preparing the professional or academic laborer in the past—be it in pastoral care or in biblical philology—which coincided with the specialized labor in other fields and a national economy that supported this specialized labor, no longer holds.

Globalization has given way to world systems, world economy, global frames of knowledge, and a demand for new ways of knowing and understanding. The emphasis on specialization has been supplanted by the urgent need to prepare persons to participate in this global setting. Educational institutions themselves must become "markets of exchange." Whether engaged in the study of complex moral issues, questions of doctrine, or a challenging biblical passage, students are constantly exchanging information across national, ethnic, cultural, sexual, and class borders and attending to cultural transactions at the heart of these exercises. Instead of mastering a specialized pool of knowledge, students are expected to construct frames of knowledge from the proliferation of local particularities and cultural diversity now resident in our classrooms. In addition to understanding their own religious traditions, students need to cross traditions without a fixed position about meaning. Instead of acquiring a body of religious knowledge, students learn how religious knowledge transmutes into forms of political power and back again. In concert with appreciating the biblical text as a confessional or aesthetic work, students must learn how the active reception of confessional or aesthetic works can equal the passive reception of oppressive or hegemonic power.

The appeal of a New Historicism in biblical studies is more than the product of a theoretical argument in literary studies. Rather, its rise is seeded by changes in the very institutions where it is being practiced. Exchange and negotiation across the cultural histories and identities of seminary and university populations concerning the cultural histories and identities in the biblical writings are at the heart of our efforts. We cannot do otherwise in a world where boundary crossing has become requisite not only for economics, politics, and communication, but for ministry, for biblical and theological understandings, and for knowledge itself.

3
On the Differences between Historicism and the New Historicism

Discussions of New Historicism often begin by mapping its differences from historicism as we have known it.[1] Well prepared to participate in this practice, I begin first by noting what is at stake in elaborating such sharp distinctions. The biblical guild, like the larger academy itself, is a market of exchange, or what Frederic Jameson describes as the academic marketplace under late capitalism.[2] Within this market economy, we exchange ideas, promote our interpretations, advance our methods, and compete with our theories. We appeal to consumers by commodifying the "new" and pointing out the advantages of our offerings over their current reigning counterparts. The same is true with New Historicism, we show, by its differences with what is practiced and how it addresses some of the shortcomings of historicism in the past. As customer awareness increases (usually that of our colleagues and our students) by virtue of our commercial practices in advertising these "wares," it behooves us to exercise greater savvy in proffering our goods.

So, I do not begin this discussion immediately contrasting a New Historicism with a caricatured "old" Historicism. Though ultimately intending to advertise New Historicism as an alternative to what has been practiced, I anticipate that a frontal attack on historicism as we have known it might offend and thus drive away some of my would-be customers. Instead, I enlist what I hope to be a more subtle tactic. I begin by pointing out the fundamental commonality, the essential kinship between my product, New Historicism, and historicism, its predecessor—namely, their mutual regard for the past and its relevance for the present.

RELEVANCE OF THE PAST FOR THE PRESENT

Historicism and New Historicism both view the past as irreplaceably valuable in affording us insight and knowledge about how we live in the present. Individually and collectively, we draw upon the past to shape our identity and destiny in the future as well as to apprehend meaning and self-understanding in the present. In *The Idea of History* published in the mid 1950s, R. G. Collingwood designated "human self-knowledge" as the very reason for doing history at all.[3] This objective has been reiterated down through the ages and across numerous disciplines that make use of history.

In biblical studies, the importance of studying the past is well-represented in the role that historical exegesis has had in the past two centuries. The Enlightenment and its legacy elevated historical studies to the status of "essential" for any credible interpretation of the Bible. This significance was reinforced and furthered magnified, particularly in this century, when tied to the theological enterprise that concerns some scholars. Not only does history inform our self-understanding, but it has been often defended as the very foundation for knowledge of God as well. A Christian faith founded upon a *Heilsgeschichte,* or salvation history, and upon theological tenants derived from that history, cannot ignore the past. Understanding divine activity in the present always invites remembering and interpreting God's salvific deeds in the past. The Old Testament, often spoken about as the account of salvation history, mandates this kind of inquiry. In the 1930s, a debate between Walter Eichrodt and Otto Eissfeldt on the role of history in the construction of a biblical theology spawned an array of positions on the subject that eventually erupted as a crisis. Still unresolved, the role of history in a biblical theology remains a point of contestation today.[4]

At the heart of the debate lies the assumption that in biblical studies, as in other disciplines, the past matters for the present. This conviction of the relationship between past and present in biblical studies was well articulated in Krister Stendahl's classic essay on biblical theology. He argued the importance and priority of determining "what the text meant" in order to accurately apprehend "what the text means."[5] And, of course, "what the text meant" required attention to the composition and reception of the text in its ancient context as prelude to grasping its significance for the present.

Recent reception theory and reader-response criticism, however, has made these distinctions all but indefensible. And though the distinction between what the text meant and what the text means wanes, the conviction that the past matters for the present endures. Scholars are acutely aware of the problems and questions that surround the matter of doing history. Whether it is the question of the existence of an ancient Israel, the challenge of reconstructing Israelite religion, or determining exactly what *is* historical exegesis of the text, scholars persist in their efforts. Though inheritors of these dilemmas, students are still taught to attend to the background of a text and its relevant context (among other things) in preparing to preach and teach the Word for today. Hence, despite its methodological problems, the conviction that history matters for the present still governs our research and instruction.

In a similar vein, New Historicists see their historical projects as intimately tied to the present and invaluable for serving the interests and needs of their own setting in life. It is no secret that attention to history as signifying what we call "the past" discloses its real significance in and for the present and the future. These narratives about the past are often conceived to address, directly or indirectly, the issues and anxieties of current realities. Either by analogy or causally, the past is tied to the present and can be mined for the lessons it teaches.

But New Historicists go even further. They suggest that the distinction maintained between past and present is less real than we think. Stephen Greenblatt notes that his fascination with Renaissance literature "seemed to be powerfully linked to the present both analogically and casually."[6] He reflects further on this connection: "this double link at once called forth and qualified my value judgments: called them forth because my response to the past was inextricably bound up with my response to the present."[7] In addressing those who work in the humanities, Montrose challenges us "to disabuse students of the notion that history is what's over and done with" and to awaken in them the realization "that the forms and pressures of history are made manifest in their subjective thoughts and actions, in their beliefs and desires."[8] Hence, in New Historicism as in conventional historicism, the study of the past is intimately caught up with and embedded in the present and is immensely valuable for grappling with and informing the quest for insight and self-understanding in our current reality. But out of this shared assumption arise differences whereby New Historicism moves away from conventional historicism and its theoretical base. These include the following: (1) the understanding of the past and its history; (2) the disciplinary arenas and the practitioners that work in them; and (3) the relation between historical context and literary text.

THE PAST AND ITS HISTORY

Concerned about the past and its influence upon the present, both parties are interested in texts, artifacts, and evidence, as well as in producing narratives that grapple with this "pastness." But the heart of this common pursuit, "the past," is in the first order what separates them. To some degree, historicism has traditionally proceeded with the confidence of a quantifying science. It views the past as retrievable, and in some instances even unproblematically knowable. While the evidence may need to be discovered, excavated, translated, and reconstructed, the confidence in the presumed outcome supports and insures these labors, that "what once was" can be known.

On the other hand, New Historicism, with its postmodern connections, manifests an underlying skepticism about knowledge of the past. It considers the past as forever past. History does not report the facts. Rather, it attends to what once was, but always with the awareness that it is "after the fact." In their introduction to a collection of New Historicist essays, Jeffrey Cox and Larry Reynolds put it succinctly. The New Historicism "rejects the idea of 'History' as a directly accessible, unitary past, and substitutes for it the conception of 'histories', an ongoing series of human constructions, each representing the past at particular present moments for particular present purposes."[9] Hence, what we represent as the past, is just that, *our* representation. As *our* representation, the past is intimately tied to the present and the powerful tendency to appropriate the past in terms of the present.[10]

From these two divergent notions of the past spring different understandings of "history." The history inherent in most historicisms stems from reconstructing the events, lives, and chronologies of bygone eras. It may work to reconstitute texts and evidence from these periods or it may labor to reconstruct whole sociocultural contexts. Faithful to both these objectives and to its roots in the Germanic *geschichtliche* schools, historical criticism in biblical studies has proceeded along these lines. Some scholars work in the arena of text criticism in order to establish the most original or defensible text. Source, form, and redaction (tradition) critical studies also contribute by tracing the development of the individual traditions, whole books, or even the canon itself. Other historical critics wrestle with actual bits and pieces of archaeological evidence and artifacts as they puzzle over the architecture of original structures such as David's Citadel, strive to trace the contour of the outer wall of Jerusalem, or map the layout of an entire settlement like Qumran. Others employ social or political theory, or enlist anthropological comparisons in sketching the social, political, or economic profiles of whole societies, be it exilic Israel or the Greco-Roman world.

Under the aegis of historical criticism, biblical scholars have produced a vast array of different and often conflicting proposals. For example, the long-reigning explanation of the Pentateuch's compositional history, the Documentary Hypothesis, is now widely challenged and in some circles has actually been permanently dethroned. Regarding the account of the conquest of Canaan in Joshua 1–20, claims range from the assertion that archaeological evidence supports the biblical story to the argument that the entire biblical tradition is divorced from any historical reality. And while no dominant alternative to biblical history itself has arisen in its place, Robert Carroll notes that "the air is full of noises and many different historians have been busy producing massive tomes on the history of 'early' Israel."[11] In the wake of endless hypotheses, historical studies has become the target of sustained criticism.

Since the mid 1960s, a growing skepticism has challenged these claims, the methods, and what some consider to be the scant evidence upon which many projects were founded. At the center of the discussions has been the question of the historical value of the biblical books themselves. Can they be counted as sources for reconstructing ancient Israel, or are they to be discounted as legendary materials? Are they to be read against the backdrop of history, or are they historical books themselves? This debate continues to intensify even today.

As confidence in historical studies dwindled, interest in literary studies and the promises of new criticism arose. The story is a familiar one. Historical criticism's preoccupation with context was replaced by formalist focus upon texts. The concerns of historical exegetes with the author and intentionality were supplanted by fixation upon the reader and his or her contemporality. From close readings to structuralist analysis, from poststructuralism's critique to deconstructionists' modes of interpretation, all roads seem to lead away from the sovereignty of historical kinds of inquiry toward what today has developed into the currency of postmodernist approaches.[12]

Ironically, the journey that literary approaches have traveled, from new criticism to postmodernism as alternative to historical inquiry, has led us back to the question of history. Fred Burnett notes, "far from being the threat many historians believe them to be, postmodern and poststructural ways of reading have provided the condition or possibility for rethinking 'history' and how it should be written."[13] Further, the postmodern assertion that both the text and the reader are culturally and historically constrained makes abandoning historical inquiry an impossibility. But the postmodernists' self-conscious grappling with theory requires the historian to rethink some key premises and assumptions of their discourse. In particular, the distinctions (text/context, fact/fiction, objective/subjective, author/reader, past/present) by which they distinguish what they do from what literary critics do must be reconsidered.[14] With these revisions, what appeared to be a turn away from historical studies by literary critics may warrant a return—but in the guise of a New Historicism.

Acknowledging the radical otherness of the past, New Historicism works with a notion of history that reminds us of its ties to postmodernity. Its skepticism regarding knowledge about the past coincides with New Historicism's views of "evidence" about the past. Texts, artifacts, shards, non-literary pieces—all the remains that historians consider as the data from which to apprehend the past—New Historicism treats as representations or remakings of the past. The words or textualized traces of the past have all but replaced worlds of the past. Constructions of the past that result from this evidence, namely history, as well as the evidence itself, are defined as texts. The past always assumes a textualized form, be it a poem, artifact, shard, court list, or biblical story. Thus it is the terrain for literary study. Moreover, it is, in its textualized form, as Peter Barry notes, "'thrice-processed': first through the ideology, or outlook, or discursive practices of its own time, then through those of ours, and finally through the distorting web of language itself."[15]

Less interested in how the evidence serves to apprehend what once was, New Historicism is more apt to be captivated by how these textualized traces

28

came to be produced. Turning attention to the elements that contributed to this "processing," New Historicism necessarily considers the ideological forces instrumental in the remaking or representing of the past. For example, Greenblatt studies Shakespearean plays in such a way as to illuminate the power relations in the courts, colonial society, church, and military administration of Renaissance culture. Over the course of the twentieth century, biblical studies itself has paid increasing attention to ideological forces at work in the compositional history in the biblical tradition as well as in the biblical world itself. As early as the promulgation of the Documentary Hypothesis at the turn of the century, scholars were concerned with the sociopolitical influences at work in the development of a J tradition from the South over and against an E tradition for the North. Prompted by Martin Noth's *Überlieferungsgeschichtliche Studien*, scholars have argued for promonarchic versus anti-monarchic sentiments operative ideologically in different eras that thus motivated the composition of different segments of the Deuteronomistic History.[16] Influenced by recent theorists outside the biblical field, scholars now produce complex analysis of ideological forces at work in the production of biblical texts. Norman Gottwald draws upon Terry Eagleton's categories of materialist literary criticism in an ideological analysis of Isaiah 40–55.[17] Gottwald demonstrates that for the former Judahite ruling class who were faced with extinction in their exilic Babylonian environs, Isaiah 40–55 serves as a weapon of struggle to preserve their sociocultural identity, as well as to instill confidence in a political future. Hence biblical studies, like New Historicism, has concerned itself with ideological influences in the production of text.

In addition, New Historicism assumes that its own representations of the past and that of other interpretive traditions preceding it contribute to the processing of the past. Thus, it considers the ideological uses for which the present enlists some of these versions of the past, as well as the ideological influences operative in those eras that produced these interpretive traditions. All this supposes a kind of history in literary studies that offers a new relationship to our past.[18] And it is this relation of past to ourselves in the present, along with attention to the ideological forces and influences inherent in the production, that distinguishes New Historicism from the customary modes of historical research.[19]

29

DISCIPLINARY ARENAS AND THEIR PRACTITIONERS

These different conceptualizations of history explain why historicism and New Historicism take up residence in different disciplinary arenas. Faithful to the title, historicism conducts itself within the discipline of history or historiography. As history works to define and relate the evidence discovered, an ever-growing repository of solid "facts" confirms the success of its labors. These facts, in turn, serve the interests of other disciplines. In literary studies, they are drawn upon by critics in order to establish the contexts. These in turn illuminate the background against which literary texts can be read and understood. Implicit in this way of proceeding is the assumed difference between literary and non-literary evidence, literature and history, literary critic and historian.

These distinctions are reinforced by historicism's identification with the empirical sciences both in mind-set and method. Like the order that governs the natural world, an order structures the interrelation and succession of the events that history records. As patterns of cause and effect dictate the unfolding of the relation between elements in nature, so, too, such chains of cause and effect situate and explicate the unfolding of events in histories. A commitment to chronology structures and organizes the events in the diachronic order in which they are deemed to have occurred.

In biblical studies, these organizational frameworks often begin with large periods of biblical history—the Patriarchal Period, Conquest, Era of the Judges, Monarchy, Divided Kingdom, and so on. These designations already spotlight some aspects, events, and groups of the past while others are left in the shadows. Next, events such as battles, land exchanges, treaties, journeys, building projects, and the rise and fall of kings constitute the substructure of the larger periods. In good historical fashion, evolutionary links, diachronic lines of progression, the privileging of origins, and chains of cause and effect craft the continuum along which Israel's past unfolds. Finally, the individual biblical traditions and the established intention of authors of various strands of tradition are mounted upon this unfolding picture, reinforcing, finalizing, or sometimes even contradicting the logic of its chronological unfolding.

The context narrated by this kind of historical reconstruction is stable. Hints of chaos, contingency, or problematic relations between happenings is uncharacteristic or even out of place in this kind of writing. In genre, the account of the reconstructed past identifies itself as historical narrative, not literature. Rhetorically, such writing equates what is written with factuality, not fiction. As narrative product it identifies with reality, not interpretation. And in tone, it conveys impartiality, not passion. In fact, any suggestion of the historian's hand as creative agent—authoring, designing, or positioning the parts, players, or progression of what unfolds—is out of place.

Instead, these historians function as guardians of the past, restorers of bygone eras, preservers of someone else's work. From an outsiders' assessment, they might even be thought of as self-effacing, relegating their own interests or contemporary issues to the sidelines while working to recover what once was. Faithful to the principles of historiography, they strive to be as impartial and as objective as possible in reconstituting another's text or a historical era.

In biblical studies, these scholars function as invaluable custodians of a past and of a tradition. They work and rework biblical history with each new piece of evidence. They work and rework the text anew with each new philological disclosure. They trace changes in the development of the text, seeking out motivation of involved authors down through the centuries. They define settings for the composition of the text and study the political, and most recently, the ideological framework that sketches a backdrop against which the text is read. While recognizing the impossibility of total objectivity, they endeavor to recover and preserve the most impartial and reliable construction of Israel's past. While their own descriptions narrate this past, they strive to let the evidence speak for itself. Accuracy of their work rests on the lucidity of their arguments, and the degree of detachment and objectivity they can bring to their work.

Conceived as a literary-critical movement in departments of literary studies, New Historicism conducts itself in quite a different manner. First, it resides within the discipline of literary studies, not history. However, it is a literary approach with the traditional boundaries redrawn and the disciplinary holding gates burst open. Unlike approaches to texts that have dominated the last thirty years of literary studies, New Historicism turns its attention to history. Recognition of the cultural and social embeddedness and specificity of all forms of literature prompts this about-face. At the same time, New Historicism's swerve toward history is qualified. While New Historicists do not deny the chronology of past events, they see no reason to structure their narratives along these lines. The organization of chronological accounts along a particular continuum or by means of a particular notion or pattern is preconceived. For example, historical progression occurs by means of the programs of those in power: heads of tribes, judges, or kings. Historical progression can also unfold by virtue of battles fought and battles won. Or historical progression can be organized by peasants who lost their jobs or with reference to women and their contributions to society. In addition, the juxtaposition of literary events from different periods can reveal more about them temporally than when they are forced to narrate their own sequence. Hence, New Historicists organize their stories in whatever way they can disclose possible insights about the temporal reality of these texts. Second, New Historicism rejects the notion of history as equal to the real or lived experience. It refuses to draw sharp distinctions between history and fiction. Consistent with these views, it recognizes historical representation as related on some level to the historians' own interests or subjectivities.

New Historicism's qualification of what is meant by histories begins to look a lot like what is meant by "literary text." But its views of literary texts are qualified too, especially regarding those characteristics that set it apart from historical kinds of evidence. New Historicism rejects notions of literary texts as self-contained linguistic artifacts. Instead, in New Historicism, literature as cultural representation replaces literature as autonomous art. Ideological analysis of discursive cultural practices replaces formalist or aesthetic analysis of texts. And how these texts shape and are reshaped by their social context is in part tied to the critic's own self, a self that is culturally and socially constrained as well.

In New Historicism, this repositions the literary critics and how they view themselves in relation to their subjects. Moreover, it also signals yet another contrast with historicism and its practitioners. The aims or even claims of neutrality and objectivity associated with historians contrast sharply with the self-conscious involvement and even playfulness of New Historicists. Believing that every construction of the past is governed and integrally bound up with the present, New Historicists unabashedly insert themselves in their work. In forging their interpretations, they ignore what has been assumed as the differences between past and present. Instead, they make connections between the cultural products under investigation, other artifacts or texts of that time, intervening interpretive traditions, and elements of their own life circumstances. Interested in studying the "re-makings of the past," they understand that their own project becomes another remaking. Suspicious about any claims to truth about the past, they strive instead to offer a critique of the reigning wisdom about how the past was produced.

THE RELATIONSHIP BETWEEN
HISTORICAL CONTEXT AND LITERARY TEXT

As these critics occupy different positions in relation to their work, so also does historical context assume a different relationship to literary texts. Operating within the parameters of traditional historicism, most of us are accustomed to a history that functions essentially as a backdrop when reading and interpreting literary texts. Once discovered and reconstructed, it becomes the stable point of reference against which literary texts can be anchored and read. This historical context, or as some call it, the "world behind the text," situates and clarifies the elusive references, the porous nature of literary artifacts and texts. In biblical studies, this world behind the text becomes an essential foundation upon which to fasten and argue an interpretation. For centuries, scholars' interpretive work on Daniel 1–6 or on the Book of Jonah, for example, has depended to a large extent upon the historical situatedness or context that could be credibly established for the text.

Pursuit of original or intended meaning of the literary text hinges upon establishing and defending the correct historical setting. Moreover, the concretization provided by historical context addresses or even remedies the elusiveness, instabilities, or uncertainties presented by the literary work. Consistent with this stabilization process that the historical context provides, the description of this backdrop tends to be uncomplicated, integrated, and monological, often representing a single political vision. The culture depicted therein appears to be well-organized, definable, and homogeneous. Dominant traits, ideas, offices, and mores provide its essential characteristics. Chronological enshrinements of eras such as the "Solomonic Enlightenment" or the period of the Judges further define and delimit the character of this setting. In addition, the political perspective expressed here is not only singular in nature but probably identical with that held by only one segment of the population. Moreover, this group was more than likely a dominant group, perhaps the literate class.

By contrast, New Historicists understand historical context to consist of "competing voices, values, centers of power."[20] It is made up of both dominant and subservient voices, ascending and descending energies, residual emergent and pre-emergent features. Its surface is messy and in-process. Instead of being coherent, organized, and defensible, the historical context reveals a realm "characterized by forces of heterogeneity, contradiction, fragmentation and difference."[21] Hence, of most interest in New Historicist studies are the textual echoes of these contests, power struggles, social ruptures, and dissonance.

In addition, when New Historicism makes these contestations of historical context the center of its inquiry, it does not define context as encompassing only the setting or era of the writing. It also includes the context of the transmission, reading, and interpreting. Thus as Jerome McGann notes, New Historicism as a critical perspective concerns itself with three distinct foci: "the work at its point of origin, the work through its subsequent transmissions, and the work situated in the immediate field of a present investigation."[22]

For New Historicists, histories are themselves constrained and embedded in the social material world that represent them in words, as well as in the social material world that receives them. Disclosed here are the mutually constructive as well as reciprocal relations between the social and discursive realms, between the historical and the literary activities. Montrose's chiastic formulation "the historicity of texts and the textuality of history" expresses and illuminates this reciprocity and kinship. Explaining what he means by such an utterance, Montrose writes,

> By its acknowledgment of the *historicity of texts:* the cultural specificity, the social embedment, of all modes of writing—not only those texts that critics study but also the texts in which they study them; and on the other hand, by its acknowledgment of the *textuality of history:* the unavailability of a full and authentic past, a lived material existence, that has not already been mediated by the surviving texts of the society in question—those "documents" that historians construe in their own texts, called "histories," histories that necessarily but always incompletely construct the "History" to which they offer access.[23]

For New Historicism, the distinction between history and text or literature and historical context collapses. Instead of the historical context being sketched as representing one social or political position, it is instead crafted as a site of social unrest or locus of struggle. In turn, the literary text is not read in light of the context or representing the historical complex; rather "its writing and publication are themselves aspects of the struggles."[24]

This symbiosis between historical context and literary text also extends to the mechanics of writing. History, because it involves someone's retelling of the past, is itself "text." Moreover, history makes use of the same literary conventions as literature. Both enlist a plot format by which to frame and organize events. Both make use of genres, poetics, and stylistics in composing an intelligible narrative for readers of a particular era. Biblical histories are especially illustrative of this process.

Hayden White, the most eloquent spokesperson for this view, defines the kinship between history and literature thus. In contrast to a purely descriptive science, history provides "a plot structure for a sequence of events so that their nature as a comprehensible process is revealed by their figuration as *a story of a particular kind*."[25]

Seeing history as a text like other literary texts complicates the matter of how to define its relationship to literature. If it does not serve as backdrop or scenery against which to contextualize literature, then how are we to conceptualize this relationship? New Historicists view the relationship between history and literature, between historical context and literary text, as mutually fashioning and as a dynamic interchange. As history constitutes what we mean by a literary work, so too literary texts help to constitute what we mean by history. Biblical texts do not passively reflect actual events or uncover timeless universal truths. Instead they shape our view of historical reality and influence what reality itself might be. In this sense, the biblical narratives—like the historical narratives about ancient Israel—are often sites of struggle to interpret and to control what we might refer to as the politics of representation.

4
Recurring Characteristics of New Historicist Studies

Most studies in this series, *Guides to Biblical Scholarship*, devote one chapter to the stages involved in the method of interpretation under discussion. In what has become an almost prescribed format of these volumes, the steps of the interpretive procedure under investigation are enumerated, defined, and clarified. In each of the first three volumes of the series, the authors established this precedent. In his volume, Gene Tucker defined four progressive steps for conducting form criticism.[1] In his essay, Norman Habel offered a synopsis of key features for analysis when doing literary criticism.[2] Finally, Walter Rast earmarked four foci in conducting tradition criticism in his piece.[3] As the framework of the series became defined by these first three studies, subsequent volumes followed suit. In *The Historical-Critical Method*, one of the earliest volumes, Edgar Krentz enumerated the steps for external criticism of the "origin and integrity of a work" as preliminary to carrying out the procedures for internal criticism, "the determination of the original sense and the evaluation of the competence and honesty of the witness."[4] Some twenty years later, Mark Powell remained faithful to the expectation by setting forth a discussion of key features for analysis that constitute the interpretive method of narrative criticism.[5]

New Historicism's inclusion in a series that assumes and defines method in such a clear-cut fashion is somewhat of an oddity and presents a twofold challenge. First, as both a product and extension of the theoretical ferment of the past two decades, New Historicism raises questions about the very notion of method itself. This suspicion, however, does not originate with New Historicists. It is a question that has surfaced in the larger academy as well as in biblical studies in recent years. Within biblical studies, scholars

37

such as John Barton reject the claims that the numerous critical ways we claim to read texts are really methods or sets of procedures insuring a certain outcome. "Biblical methods are theories, rather than methods: theories that result from the formalizing of intelligent intuitions about the meaning of biblical texts."[6] But because the theory is logically subsequent to the intuition about meaning, New Historicism dodges this qualification as well. Its kinship with theory, if at all, is with postmodern partners and the questions they raise about theory and method. Like other disciplines operative under the currents of postmodernism, New Historicism resists systems or methodological ways of proceeding that flatten incongruities, unify differences, obscure particularities, or ignore those elements that seem to obstruct or resist claims of otherwise integral schemes or structures in texts.

Second, characterized by its stance as amethodological, any attempt to explain what New Historicism is and how it does what it does guarantees an involvement in a self-contradictory feat. New Historicism has been characterized as a sensibility governed by a set of working assumptions about texts. These assumptions, along with various recurring features, shape and define the collective ethos by which a growing group of practitioners read and interpret texts.

Despite this rejection of methodological categorization and theoretical specification under the rubric of "postmodernity," the familiar nomenclature of steps, categories, and stages still tempts even the most well-informed of its advocates. In offering an exposition of New Historicism as characteristically unmethodological, H. Aram Veeser observes "moments" that can be thought of as exemplary of New Historicist "strategy."[7] In his analysis of the essay, "Marlowe and the Will to Absolute Play," Veeser notes five moments that stage Stephen Greenblatt's exposition here: anecdote, outrage, resistance, containment, and autobiography.[8] Skeptics might be quick to criticize that steps masquerade as "moments" and methodological approach as "strategy" here. It is as if New Historicists themselves find it difficult to talk about what they are up to in working on texts without resorting to the nomenclature of "steps," "strategy," and "stages." However, these "moments" were never intended as a methodological road map to New Historicist studies. That Susan Lochrie Graham and Stephen D. Moore pick up on these "moments" and employ them as coy parody in structuring their New Historicist project "The Quest of the New Historicist Jesus" suggests the problem.[9]

Apprehending a way of reading that we cannot map presents real difficulties. First, the fixed set of questions or operations that guide both the writer and reader do not exist. The step-by-step format or formulaic set of questions that navigate a particular kind of reading and instruct others in that way of proceeding are absent. The criteria that methodological identification affords for evaluating a reading is nonexistent. Most significantly, the distance and even the academic defense that methods afford when justifying an interpretive outcome have been compromised. As New Historicists, we, rather than an innocuous method, become more directly responsible for the outcome. Perhaps that is the real contribution of New Historicism. It not only requires that we rethink how we study texts in history and history in texts, it also warrants our acknowledgment that responsibility for the consequences of interpretive outcomes rests squarely on our shoulders.

Although no blueprint or prescription exists for how to proceed in doing New Historicism, the situation is not hopeless. Several features recur often enough in both Renaissance studies and in the growing number of projects in biblical studies to suggest characteristic proclivities of the enterprise.

Some of these have already been considered in the chapter on the "Differences between Historicism and a New Historicism." Four others that are also frequently recognized across New Historicist essays include: (1) ways of reading that look less at the center and more at the borders of the literary domain, (2) attention to the struggle in texts, (3) identifying and defining the interests and forces of the past and of the present that crisscross and rebound across these representations, (4) exploring narrative as a vast intertext, "a mosaic of citations (where) every text is the absorption and transformation of other texts."[10]

1. Ways of reading that look less at the center and more at the borders of a literary work

Turning away from pursuits of rhetorical integrity or literary unity, New Historicism attends to the cracks, the underside, and signs of disarray latent in a work. Convinced that "whole readings" are but a self-satisfying illusion, New Historicism opts for more fragmentary kinds of considerations. Resisting the tendency to integrate dominant images, dialogues, and characters into a single master discourse, it attends to fleeting references, incongruities, or unanswered questions resident at the borders or margins of the text.[11] For example, instead of focusing on whether Josiah's religious reform (2 Kings 24) was religiously grounded or politically motivated, New Historicism might wonder about the peasants who lost their jobs when the local shrines were dismantled. Instead of being captivated by the details of this king's centralization of cult, it would inquire about how hierarchical forms of power become the enabling conditions of such detailed representations.

Attention to these borders often discloses a complicated past that resists the coherence of reigning historical reconstructions, while unaddressed questions lurking in the margins disrupt the integrity of unified readings. In lieu of producing an outcome that conforms to the monological tendencies of traditional historical or even literary interpretation, New Historicism uncovers "a past of competing voices, values, and centers of power. . . ."[12] Lori Rowlett's study of texts in the Book of Joshua is illustrative. Instead of focusing on the royal propaganda so well documented in the literature, Rowlett considers "the process of marginalization within the text and how the rhetoric of violence expressed in military language is used to set and negotiate boundaries of inclusion, exclusion, and marginality."[13] For example, she studies how the repetitive emphasis on "all Israel" at recurring rituals and assemblies associated with warfare throughout Joshua not only serves to promote clearly defined and unequivocal identity; it also raises the question whether the emphasis on "all Israel" might indicate that lack of identity or confusion of group identity by "outsiders" is of concern. As New Historicism maps and investigates these traces of conflict and confusion, it must redefine and reposition the relationship of literary text to context.

Literature is not the reflection of the beliefs, values, or habits of the age in which it is produced. Such a notion is considered deceptive and served as the impetus for the rejection of the question of context by formalists, structuralists, and even deconstructionists. Like its predecessors, New Historicism recoils from this view of literature in relation to context. Unlike these earlier alternatives to traditional literary historicism, however, it deems context essential for the study of texts, the very condition without which other forms of study cannot meaningfully take place.

This re-admittance of context to literary discussions, however, demands re-visioning the relationship between text and context. For New Historicism, texts are constitutive of, as well as constituted by, context. They contribute to and are shaped by social forces. Moreover, language, a socially collective construction itself, serves as essential building material. Consequently, New Historicism assumes the "social presence to the world of the literary text and the social presence of the world in the literary text."[14] It refuses to privilege reality over text, instead understanding that reality is constructed by texts. The real world or context is constantly being formed and transmitted through textual and visual discourse. Worlds have become words. What we count as the reality, as the world of the past, is formed through what is represented.

Thus the question of how "reality" or "context" relates to the text—how the individual biblical story relates to the real ancient world—raises the wrong question. Instead, New Historicism considers what is being promoted and what is being constrained in the representation. Who is being silenced or resisted by the dominant voice in the discourse? What is being concealed by that which is being revealed? What is being endorsed and at whose expense? As one can see, attention to the margins—to the borders—reveals biblical texts to be more than fine literature. The dynamic of contestation evident there defines these writings along with other literary works as sites of struggle warranting a different kind of consideration.

2. Attention to the struggle in texts

Compared to the numerous and sometimes dirty political reports about the "real" world, biblical texts as well as other literary pieces are typically thought of as harmless, and therefore beside the point. In fact their status as art or literature and indeed as sacred Scripture endows them their characterization as sanitized and as removed from the nitty-gritty concerns of human existence. Thus they are often viewed as a tranquil retreat or refuge from the domestic demands, social strife, or economic challenges that rule our lives.

Whether in writing, music, painting, architecture, or the Bible itself, this separation of the arts from other forms of knowledge and human enterprise can be traced to the Enlightenment period. The Enlightenment bestowed upon us the realm of the "aesthetic"—an autonomous discursive sphere that redefined, arranged, and influenced knowledge according to principles different from other arenas. The rearrangement of the university disciplines into the "Arts and Sciences" is a most compelling indication of this influence.

The field of biblical studies itself has identified with the university discipline of the arts (literature, linguistics, etc.), thus adopting both its theory and methods. Moreover, the aesthetic has been assumed as a defensible domain in which to ground biblical interpretations. As literature, the biblical texts are assumed to possess a literary integrity, deep structures, and rhetorical unity. As autonomous art, they have even been interpreted at times without reference to anything outside themselves. Were it not for the outcry of feminist readers, Third World critics, or racial and ethnic minority readers who experience the damning social consequences of some of these aesthetically autonomous readings, we might have never questioned the very existence of the aesthetic.

The invention of the aesthetic has not only materialized as new and separate divisions among university disciplines; it has also masked recognition of the role these texts play in promoting and maintaining social divisions. Furthermore, the persistent assertion of the aesthetic domain, when girded with political or religious authority, disguises the role that literature, art, and music play in constituting social life, social processes, and social hierarchies.

What if works of art, even the biblical texts, are not privatized, separated, or dissociated from the real world? What if, rather, they are involved with it? What if, in fact, they are instrumental in defining what is real? Influenced by the work of feminists whose critique of the representations of women in texts has shown how these representations have, in fact, constituted the "real," New Historicism rejects the separation of the material from the aesthetic domain.[15] Feminist critics theorize that the relation between the material/political world on the one hand and the textual/representational world on the other closely and mutually fashion one another. As noted earlier, New Historicism, influenced by Foucault, assumes a concept of discourse that comingles the linguistic, cultural, sociopolitical, and material realms. And it is amidst this comingling that echoes of struggle can be heard.

Instead of reading literature against a historical backdrop or comparing it to art, New Historicism views literature as it does all texts—whether they are novels, buildings, religious rubrics, film, legislation, or institutional regulations. All texts are caught up in the complex and contestatory processes by which a society defines and maintains its organization, institutions, as well as its self-understanding. As such, societies are caught up in the struggles whereby one segment of culture defines itself as dominant. In the process, they construct discourses that distinguish them from a subservient segment of culture defined as "the other."

Edward Said was one of the first to illustrate this in his study of colonialist discourses. Here he exposes how the Orient has been made to represent "the other" in Western minds and culture and how the representation affects the mentality of Westerners.[16] Such discourse sets up a dichotomy that presents the colonizer as rational, male, civilized, and parental over and against the colonized who is irrational, female, uncivilized, and childish. Here the terms of discourse serve to reinforce the domination by colonizer as well as limit the strategies of liberation for the colonized. What the mimetic feature discloses is not *reality* but the struggle involved in the construction of a certain reality by a dominant group.

In an article in *The New Yorker,* Greenblatt discerns this struggle in his assessment of something as innocuous as the popular household magazine, *National Geographic.*[17] Despite *National Geographic's* well-known, nonpartisan, and nondominant editorial policy committed to only kindly representations of the world, "the photographing of natives has an air of colonial acquisitiveness—of the accumulation of cultural loot."[18] Greenblatt notes that these representations along with other such collections (he cites, for example, Ed Stricken's now long-published 1955 exhibit, "Family of Man") depict not the reality but the struggle. "The universal and its lackey, the aesthetics, are revealed with numbing regularity to be agents of those in power."[19]

Similarly, a story that narrates and celebrates a monarch's wisdom such as the biblical tale of "Solomon and the Two Mothers" (1 Kings 3:16-28) probably represents reality in a way that serves the interests of dominant culture. Girded with the gift of wisdom bestowed by none other than God, the king adjudicates between two women subjects arguing before him. In contrast to the one woman's frantic, wordy oration and the forensic deadlock evoked when both women speak, the king practices an economy of words. In Hebrew, his two-worded command, "Bring me the sword" (3:24), not only elicits an immediate response of obedience but also forcibly ruptures the impasse of the women's verbose exchanges. While the women speak more words than the king, he holds the power of speech. While the women are incapable of resolving their differences, his words dislodge the deadlock. Thus, this contrast in characterization between the women and the king suggests the struggle.

Also, the depiction of these subjects as women and then as harlots contrasts sharply with, and distances them from, the depiction of the sovereign as male and as "wise king." Here, the biblical text, too, participates in constructing and reinforcing a version of reality that represents dominant culture within which members of a subservient culture understand themselves. Furthermore, we might ask why women here and elsewhere in the biblical tradition (for example, 2 Kings 6:24-33) are depicted at odds with one another in stories that address and illustrate the sovereignty of kings.[20] Or to put it another way, do women working together pose a threat to maintaining the hierarchical elevation of sovereigns? But the struggle in texts is not confined to the works themselves. Those who read, interpret, and preach the biblical texts down through the ages participate in these contestations.

3. Attention to the interests and forces that crisscross and rebound across cultures and across generations

Some have observed that there is something inherently odd if not outright contradictory about the label "New Historicism." The word "history" conjures up images of what is old, what has been before, what is past. "New," on the other hand, signals the novel, what is to come, what we can expect in the future.[21] In addition, New Historicism arose amongst a group of literary critics who claimed to be committed to making a difference in the present. Though trained to work in the sanitized confines of the aesthetic realm, these practitioners refused to engage in a discipline or practice unrelated to the here and now. For this generation, whom Stanley Fish calls "the young and the restless," failure to connect the present with the past seemed not only worthless, but had consequences for the future.[22] Thus, the past, present, future, and their inevitable interconnections frame the purview of New Historicists. In his discussion of Ezra Pound's *Cantos,* J. McGann elaborates these temporal connections:

> To the historicist imagination, history is the past, or perhaps the past seen in and through the present; and the historical task is to attempt a reconstruction of the past, including, perhaps, the present of the past. But the *Cantos* reminds us that the historical task involves as well the construction of what shall be possible. When we read, we construct our histories including our futures.[23]

The crux of New Historicism resides within this explicit entanglement of past, present, and future. Here, forces, interests, and concerns crisscross and rebound along the continuum of history and within the web of culture. Moreover, attention to these exchanges as we read and write about the past in the present enables us to envision change in the future. As Daniel Boyarin notes, while we cannot change the past, we can change our understanding of the past. We examine the past with the intention of seeing our own prejudices and concerns. To do so, we must first abandon one-dimensional, fixed understandings of the past. Then we strive to recover those forces or voices that oppose the dominant discourse narrating the past. In addition, we work to identify the factors and values responsible for these prejudices. Thus we encounter the past not as a burden to be discounted, but as a site where recovery of those opposing forces can help us envision and strategize prospects for change in our own time. This in turn can "put us on a trajectory of empowerment for transformation."[24]

In his discussion of New Historicism, noted literary critic Alan Liu suggests a further reason for examining the past with an eye to present "prejudices and concerns."[25] Such an exercise begins to clarify exactly what role subjectivity plays in the interpretation. It has already been noted that the role and position of New Historicism's practitioners differ from that of conventional historicists on the matter of subjectivity. Claims of subjectivity not only distinguish New Historicists from historicists in the past, but they are deemed crucial to the work of New Historicists. Exactly how this occurs invites further discussion.

When subjectivity serves as a critical tool for New Historicists, it yokes past, present, and future together while elucidating their interconnections. This stance of subjectivity materializes in two ways: at the level of the text and at the level of the reader. First, texts themselves attest to layers of subjective fashioning. Despite their appearance of fixity today, the biblical texts—along with other great works of literature—have been fashioned and refashioned by a whole series of historical transactions or negotiations. Defining and identifying these stages of composition of the biblical writings has been a persistent focus of criticism in the past century. Unlike studies by textualists and formalists that try to divorce the biblical writing from its conditions of composition, tradition and redaction critics have continued to investigate the development of texts in their contexts. For

example, the life's work of an individual scholar might have been consti-
tuted by mapping and reconstructing the corpus of a Priestly tradition in
Genesis, a pro-monarchic tradition of the Deuteronomistic History, or a
Deuteronomistic editing of Jeremiah.

It is not the question but the conclusion of these studies to which New
Historicists object. As these traditions reveal the compositional layers of a
text, they also begin being identified with a spokesperson for a dominant
group or class. Whether they are the priestly leaders of ritual and faith in the
post-exilic period, a royal class in support of kingship, or the pro-temple
group, the subjective voices of the wider community that make up the layers
of traditions often get monologized in the process. Consequently, the myr-
iad voices contributing to the development of the stories that comprise a
biblical tradition become identified with one individual or group. Yet biblical traditions are acts of engagement with a vast and diverse reality made up
of different and even opposing beliefs, values, biases, and investments. As
interpretations of that reality, the text both bears witness to, and is
imprinted with, the complexity of these fashionings.

Of course, in the case of the biblical texts, such fashioning and negotiations are rather difficult to confine to one culture or era. No text, especially
the biblical text, comes to us as autonomous or by the singular labors of one
author. It arrives bearing with it the accumulation of effects from its own
production, as well as all of its former receptions; needless to say, these two
processes are difficult to separate. As the text moves across generations, cultures, and even religious traditions, it absorbs the amalgam of these influences. For example, as the tradition of the Exodus/Settlement in the Land
has made its way across generations, it has narrated the liberation of the
Israelites from bondage at one time, the early Christians' escape from the
enemy of death at another, and most recently, the release of Latin Americans
from political oppressors. At the same time, it has also attested to the terri-
ble fate of the Canaanites, the anti-Judaic strands that helped fuel contempt
for the Jews, or even the fate of the Native Americans.

As texts are handed down, edited, and translated they are constantly
being refashioned and negotiated. Gradually, the complexity of these
interchanges span spatio-temporal webs of time, place, peoples, and culture in the ongoing production and reception of a text. Subjectivity in
production thus spills over into subjectivity in reception. This slippage not
only obscures the sharper distinctions between production and reception

and between past and present, but also between text and reader. As text interacts with reader, subjective fashioning becomes the shared condition of both.

Among New Historicists, the employment of subjectivity at the level of the reader/interpreter (self-reflexivity) is not a self-serving manipulation of the text to make it mean anything one wants. Nor is it an escape into the recesses of narcissistic self-indulgence. Instead, it invites a conscious enlistment of that which has been operative in the life of the text all along—the engagement of individual experiences, values, commitments, and concerns. These elements, constitutive of the production of text, are also operative in the reception of text. They motivate the kinds of questions we ask, the methodological choices we make, and the interpretive outcomes we produce. Used as a critical tool, self-reflexivity is a refusal to hide behind the "original author" or original audience of the text. Instead, it involves exegeting ourselves and our cultural location as we exegete the text. The kind of excavation that text and its context have enjoined in the past is now to be accompanied and intertwined with an in-depth excavation of the reader and her context. The hermeneutical models within which biblical scholars most often claim to practice our trade (that is, the Gadamerian "fusion of horizons" or the hermeneutical circle) presume this kind of equal time to both text and reader all along.

In reality, however, the thick description of text and its world have, at best, been matched by only a "thin description" (if any at all) of the reader and her context. Feminists, as well as minority readers from this country and the Third World whose work has been pivotal for New Historicists in this regard, are the exception here. They have made this journey and charted its course. They have visited the deepest recesses of self-knowledge replete with unfulfilled hopes and dreams, unthinkable memories of oppression and silencing, and the resurgent recollections of fear and pain. As a result, their readings of the biblical texts transgress the decorum and long-standing traditions of reigning interpretations, thereby exposing the power and privilege that are at stake in the maintenance of these hegemonic practices. However, many readers, particularly First World, white, upper-middle-class readers, have been slow to plumb the depths of self-understanding, avoiding acknowledgment of cherished biases, cultural location, values, and politics. At times, we have even marshaled a strong resistance to this kind of self-scrutiny, perhaps for fear of what we might find.

All this talk about self-reflexivity sounds rather grave and serious. Actually, though, there is a playfulness to the subjective engagement of New Historicists in their work. It is often unapologetically autobiographical and entertaining. Perhaps this self-exposure, if it is honest, begins to unmask some of the academic disguises we hide behind. Just as New Historicism raises questions about distinctions between past and present, between history and literature, it also wonders about the differences between the academic and the nonacademic self and the validity of the implied status and privilege of the former. The questions and concerns we have about the texts and their past are invariably the questions and concerns we share with others about ourselves and culture. This has always been the case as recent studies illustrate and make explicit.

Harold Washington investigates studies on the Hebrew sacral war tradition produced by German scholarship during the World War I era.[26] As we might expect, Washington shows that the currents and interests of German history and Prussian militarism are played out in the conclusions they forward about the biblical traditions on war. Similarly, it is not surprising that questions of gender construction and the meaning of masculinity are being asked of ancient texts such as Maccabees or the Davidic traditions by contemporary scholars concerned with issues of gender today. Stephen D. Moore and Janice Capel Anderson, in their study of Maccabees, show that the young male martyrs are subject to a very contemporary dilemma.[27] Practice of the highest form of masculinity required them to duplicate the kind of mastery to which they themselves had been subjugated. There can be little doubt that the present is very much caught up in our study of the past and the questions we raise about this past. Hence, academic work, no matter what the field, needs to be self-conscious as well as self-examining.

Cultural artifacts do not remain still but exist in time. Their construction merges with their reception. As a result, these two processes are often tightly interwoven. Moreover, in both their construction and their reception, texts are always caught up in personal, social, and institutional conflicts. As literary works continue to live, move, and have their being, their assigned meaning cannot be isolated from the uses to which persons and social organizations put those works. The perdurance of a work and its assigned meaning is a function of these appropriations. New Historicism, with its commitment to the present, attends to these forces and interests as they continue to move across generations and cultures in the production and reception of these works. In the process, these interchanges leave behind textual traces that invite consideration of the intertextual character of a work.

4. Narrative as a vast intertext

In *Postscript to the Name of the Rose,* Umberto Eco writes, "I've discovered what writers have always known (and have thereby told us again and again); books always speak of other books, and every story tells a story that has already been told."[28] Eco's observation could be applied to, and even extended by, what New Historicists do in their studies. Here, books and stories not only speak about other books and stories, but also speak about the cultural values, practices, and social relations in production and reception of texts. While desiring to restore features of "context" to interpretation, New Historicists have had to yield to the disclosures of textualist theories of the poststructuralist era. Context is always textualized and thus functions as co-text. The first frame of Montrose's now familiar chiastic formulation, "the textuality of history and the historicity of texts," aptly narrates this condition. In describing where poststructuralists have landed us, Ellen van Wolde makes a similar observation. She notes that texts are elaborately intertwined with one another.[29] Hence, in New Historicism, intertextuality moves beyond the formal confines of text-to-text relations by also attending to what Foucault notes as exchanges and mutual fashionings between and among texts and "institutions, economic and social processes, behavioral patterns, systems of norms."[30] Aware of these multiple and innate interconnections, New Historicists draw upon and explicate a vast array of intertextual ties. Links might be established between a cant term and a medical record, a play and a personal letter, a government record and a novel, a laundry list and a political speech.

In his discussion of New Historicism, Peter Barry characterizes these intertextual moves as "parallel readings of literary and nonliterary texts" in order to dethrone the privileged position of literature and place it alongside other texts.[31] But New Historicist practices involve more than juxtaposing texts in order to establish equal footing between the literary and nonliterary. Convinced that all elements of a cultural system—be it texts, artifacts, or practices—are imprinted with a "shared code, a set of interlocking tropes and similitudes that function not only as objects but as the conditions of representation,"[32] they seek out a more intimate or embedded connection between texts. Instead of side-by-side analysis of writings, New Historicism reads closely the structural connections between and among texts. In place of attending to the sequential or diachronic relation between texts or between texts and the cultural systems of their production and reception, it investigates the systemic or synchronic interweavings. For instance, Greenblatt reads a seemingly innocuous play of the Renaissance period in tandem with an unrelated document or artifact concerned with the "the horrifying colonialist policies pursued by all the major European powers of the era."[33] In the course of his readings, Greenblatt shows how the subject matter of both overlaps or intertwines with each other. Here, Shakespearean plays are shown to be "embedded in other *written texts,* such as penal, medical and colonial documents."[34]

Because no apparent organizing principle governs these relationships, nor does a methodological blueprint exist that explains how to get at them, the discovery and discussion of these interconnections have earned some pejorative characterizations. Dominick LaCapra variously describes the practice as "weak montage," "facile association," and "cut and paste bricolage."[35] But, in fact, this associative dimension of New Historicist readings is founded upon an assumption that LaCapra and other such critics would assent to, namely, that any one aspect of society is related to any other. Every text is related to other texts and other cultural practices. These interconnections, therefore, favor an intertextual analysis in the service of both history and literary studies.

In biblical studies, the intertextual character of the biblical materials tends, at first glance, to be associated with composition. The composite character of the biblical writings invites attention to the complex of sources that are woven together, edited, and identified as a text's compositional history. Whether speaking about the corpus of Pentateuchal writings, a single prophetic book like Jeremiah, or an isolated speech by Samuel in 1 Samuel, the ongoing source investigations have made clear the complex intertextual character associated with the composition of these works. Connections between Sumerian hymns and wisdom traditions, Babylonian law codes and the Covenant Code, or the Hittite treaties and Israel's covenant extend the intertextual ties to Israel's surrounding neighbors. But intertextuality refers to much more than the identification of the different traditions or common sources drawn together in the composition of a larger narrative.

The term intertextuality grows out of Julia Kristeva's reworkings of Mikhail Bakhtin's concepts of polyphony and dialogism—his terms for the multiple voicing of the text.[36] These notions divert attention away from the individual authorial process of drawing together several sources in the writing of a piece and instead focus attention upon the irreducible plurality within and behind any given text. Intertextuality constitutes the very notion of textuality. Texts are unfinished webs of textual strands constantly being worked and reworked. Dialogism refers to this enmeshment or contextually constrained character of all linguistic expression. Every word written or uttered is inextricably bound up or linked with previous utterances or uses. Every communicative act is in dialogue with its context and all its prior enactments. This echo of earlier acts, utterances, or texts in their contexts gives rise to a polyphony of voices in the texts—what Bakhtin calls the multivoiced character of texts. This is precisely what New Historicists are attending to when they focus upon the margins and listen for the struggle in texts.

Whereas Bakhtin was focused upon relations between texts and text along with text and reality, Kristeva qualifies the notion of text to include reality in the production of a work. Here the poststructuralist view of the contingent, socially constructed quality of any (linguistic) representations of "reality" is presumed. French poststructuralists, with their emphasis upon the role of reader, further broadened the scope of what is meant by intertext to include the reality of the reader. Therefore, intertext, which began with an emphasis on text production in its relation to other texts and reality, came to include text reception in every changing cultural setting. In keeping with Kristeva's expanded notion of intertextuality, New Historicists extend their interest in associative connections between texts beyond the stages of production. Greenblatt talks about "resonance" as the intertextual exchanges that continue in a work's reception. Here he means "the power of the object displayed to reach out beyond its formal boundaries to a larger world, to evoke in the viewer the complex, dynamic cultural forces from which it has emerged and for which as metaphor or more simply as metonymy it may be taken by a viewer to stand."[37] Hence, intertextuality in New Historicist studies includes dynamic interplay not only at the level of text production but also at the level of text reception.

Van Wolde has offered a most helpful discussion defining and comparing the emergent views of intertextuality along these two lines—intertextuality

as production and intertextuality as text reception.[38] Her critique of the sep-
aratist claims of these two approaches leads her to adopt an alternate model
that collaborates these two intertextual arenas and narrates well what goes
on in New Historicist studies. Drawing upon Manfred Eigen's evolutionary
model, she justifies the coexistence of intertextual moves that cycle back and
forth between text production and reader reception. Neither the absolute
arbitrariness associated with reader reception nor the absolute necessity
associated with text composition determines meaning.

Van Wolde's thoroughgoing analysis demonstrates the infinite network
of intertextual exchanges that can take place among literary texts, among literary and cultural texts, and among texts and readers in the lifespan of a
work. This enlarged and intricate sketch of intertextuality is particularly significant given what could otherwise be argued as the limitations of scholars
working on the biblical materials. Unlike scholars who have access to the
surplus of cultural texts from the Renaissance period, those working on biblical writings do not have items like Jeremiah's real estate bill of sale, medical
records from Ezekiel's time, or the personal correspondence of Deutero-
Isaiah. And while such cultural texts from the ancient Near Eastern period
would make for rich intertextual reading of the biblical material, they are in
short supply.

The biblical traditions have been handed down, rewritten, translated, and
utilized for over two thousand years. Production and reception merge as
writings are being fashioned and refashioned in the ongoing transmission,
reinscription, and reappropriation of them. In the process, the biblical
materials acquire an abundance of other intertextual cultural connections.
The strands of these intertextual skeins encircle individual communities,
entwining implementations by particular groups with those of other eras.
Over time, these strands weave back and forth across whole generations and
numerous cultures, each with its own dreams, fears, institutions, social
frameworks, political systems, and so on. Hence, what we inherit as the Bible
is not an autonomous text. Rather, the biblical tradition composes a complex networking of innumerable textual traces making possible an infinite
surplus of meaning.

Yvonne Sherwood demonstrates this cumulative quality of intertextuality in her New Historicist assessment of meta-commentary on the Book of
Jonah.[39] First, she shows how different interpretations of the book are yoked

to the intertextual exchanges between the cultural emphasis on discipline in the sixteenth century, some eighteenth-century anti-Jewish sentiments, and the fixation of the nineteenth century with "biblicized marine biology." Next she demonstrates that some twentieth-century interpretations of Jonah promoted as timeless and universal in meaning are in fact entwined with these previous intertextual products. Her observations summarize what New Historicists acknowledge about intertextuality: "Meanings of Jonah that we perpetuate today do originate in the past, but not from the fourth century, B.C.E., or whenever the book was written, but from a far more recent critical legacy."[40]

In describing where the discussion of the poststructuralists has landed us, van Wolde notes, "Everything is text and everything has become intertext."[41] Hence, any interpretation selects the intertextual connections that will be made from the infinite possibilities and thereby limits the text's possible references in order to set forth a coherent meaning. Questions about who and what controls these selections, as well as about concurrent meanings, come into play. Therefore, intertextuality as related to both production of text and reception of text always involves ideological activity. Frederic Jameson's characterization of this ideological component in interpretation as "strategies of containment" that impose meaningful structure upon the totality is apt.[42]

Thus, when practiced by New Historicists today, intertextuality as ideological activity is constrained by its own recurring features. It is concerned with margins rather than centers. The struggle in and between texts commands its attention. Finally, it studies the interests and forces of past and present that crisscross and rebound across textual representations and across the generations that are interpreting them.

5
New Historicism—
Three Illustrations

Throughout the preceding discussion, New Historicism has been characterized as a sensibility toward texts rather than a method. With its characteristic assumptions and spectrum of recurring features, New Historicism emerges more as an ethos ascribed to by its practitioners than anything approximating a method. The interest in differences, struggles, and the margins, as well as its accommodation of many different kinds of studies, numbers among the features that New Historicists themselves value. Hence, a chapter designated to set forth one text study as illustration of New Historicism contradicts some of the most fundamental notions at work here. Moreover, "an illustration" suggests a type or blueprint from which to gain access to some method or interpretive template, the very notion from which New Historicists recoil. However, to avoid illustration of what is being discussed makes the prospects of an appeal for a New Historicism in biblical studies remote.

Across this investigation, my own hunt and hope for an approach I could map, define, or make use of proved futile. However, the more New Historicists studies I encountered, the more I began to grasp the character of what this literary current is about. Determined not to be identified with a "method" and all the shortcomings that postmodern thinkers expose about such allegiances, New Historicism's practitioners alternately subscribe to ways of proceeding that cross methodological and disciplinary boundaries. They assent to working assumptions undergirding their studies rather than a blueprint about what to do and how to proceed when interpreting texts. Hence, their projects tend not to duplicate one another in strategy; rather, the diversity in ways of approaching texts tends to display a commonality of interests—issues of power, struggle, those on the margins, and the social construction of the self and the other.

In place of my thwarted expectations of "a method," I found a mind-set—one that invites various ways of assessing texts, which attends to the social consequences of what we do with texts, and which recasts history as "histories" where voices not previously audible can now be heard. Thus, in keeping with the very mind-set of New Historicism, the illustration that follows is plural. It demonstrates this New Historicist way of proceeding with its working assumptions and recurring features across three different kinds of study. By illustrating this mind-set with three distinct kinds of investigations, any inclinations to map an approach are foiled. At the same time, the prospect of seeing different kinds of studies founded on common working assumptions and interests may enhance the reader's chance of catching the spirit and partaking in the ethos of the New Historicism.

In the discussion that follows, one study attends to rabbinic literature, while the other two investigate questions in relation to Old Testament traditions. In the first piece, Daniel Boyarin offers an intertextual analysis of rabbinic writings in order to recover a usable past that can challenge current attitudes toward gender categories in contemporary Judaism.[1] In the second study, Harold Washington investigates how violence in both biblical narrative and in biblical law codes works to engender maleness.[2] His study demonstrates how this dynamic is not confined to the biblical era but crisscrosses and rebounds between ancient and contemporary society, embedding and authorizing itself in some of the most influential traditions of interpretations in which biblical studies is grounded. Finally, Yvonne Sherwood's study of three commentaries on the Book of Jonah suggests just how socially constructed and constrained readers themselves are by their social, political, and economic environs when they come to biblical texts.[3]

Across these three studies, issues of production and reception of texts are at the forefront. The kinship between interests in the present as integral to the construction of the past remains center stage and glaringly apparent. At the same time, these three studies collectively and dynamically manifest the fascination of the New Historicists with intertextual enmeshments, their concern with the margins, their fixation on contradiction and struggle, their conviction of the social embeddedness of texts, as well as their playful proclivity to spin new histories. Each is quite distinct in the questions it asks and how it conducts its investigation. Across this diversity, however, they collectively manifest the features and the potential yield for a New Historicism at this time.

DANIEL BOYARIN ON GENDER AND THE TALMUD

Daniel Boyarin sets forth a New Historicist study where the intertextual exchanges across rabbinic traditions disclose the complexity and multiplicity of discourse concerning issues of male dominance.[4] Boyarin begins with a personal admission, a feature characteristic of New Historicist studies. He says that he desires to empower a change of gender relations within the community of Jews who remain dedicated to Talmudic tradition. His immediate focus is the marginalization of women within rabbinic Judaism. More personally, he seeks a Judaism that he himself can assent to, hold on to, and pass on. Aware of the pervasiveness of androcentricism in the Talmud, Boyarin raises the question that many of us who study the biblical texts continue to ask: Why bother studying these ancient texts today?

First Boyarin lays out his assumptions regarding the androcentricism of the Talmudic traditions. We cannot change the androcentricism of the Talmud's past, but we can change our understanding of the past. Typically, the past is regarded as either a burden to be cast off or a force to be corroborated. Instead, Boyarin poses a search for a past where forces that opposed the androcentricism of the time can be recovered. This presumes a New Historicist understanding of the past as made up of competing, conflicting voices and values. He searches for evidence of this past by reading stories from the Talmud. Here, he looks for hints of struggle, contradiction, or incongruities in the texts. These serve as potential evidence of women's influence, power, autonomy, and creativity that the dominant Talmudic discourse wished to suppress. He also looks for any indications of male opposition in the Talmud itself to this dominant androcentric discourse.

Offering a brief review for readers less familiar with the contents of the Talmud, Boyarin reminds us of the character of the *aggadah* and the *halakhah*. The *aggadah*, while appearing as biographical narratives of the rabbis, is actually legendary elaborations of what some consider to be true stories. While these biographical stories become the historical backdrop for the study of the religious law *(halakhah)*, Boyarin himself views these texts as fictional.

At the same time, the *halakhah* has no authors indicated and no specified historical reference. These materials are often read and interpreted against the backdrop of the *aggadah*. Sharing the assumption of the New Historicists that all texts are socially productive and socially produced, Boyarin abandons the constricting categories of "background" and "foreground." Instead, he reads both *aggadah* and *halakhah* as deeply embedded in the social practices and historical realities. First and foremost, he understands them both as discourse. Drawing upon Michel Foucault, Boyarin contends that all literature is discourse and therefore needs to be viewed as "process rather than simply as a set of products; a process which is intrinsically social, connected at every point with mechanisms and institutions that mediate and control the flow of knowledge and power in a community."[5] Recall, as New Historicists adopt and adapt Foucault's analysis, discourse becomes not just a manner of speaking or writing but the whole "mental set" and ideology that encompasses the thinking of a particular group or society.

In his first example, Boyarin considers the story of Beruria. In the Tosefta (third-century Palestine), a woman called Beruria, daughter of Rabbi Hananya ben Tradon, offers a *halakhic* opinion on a matter that is validated by an influential tannaitic authority. The question this raises constitutes the force of this story. What if a woman had that kind of judgment and authority regarding the law? Or, as Boyarin frames the issue, "What if there were a woman like the rabbis?"[6] However, in later Babylonian texts and medieval texts, the question is muted. In a marginal gloss by Rashi to the Talmud, Beruria is reported to have committed suicide. History would draw the connection between these two fragments of tradition about this woman. Hence, her contribution to the study of Torah would be obscured by a tradition concerning the fate befitting a woman who does not know her place with regard to Torah.

Boyarin fixes attention on this story in the Tosefta. He accounts for her presence in the Tosefta by historicizing a group of men who were uncomfortable with the exclusion of women from the study of Torah. While they could not overturn society and its mores, they could at least leave behind a trace of their opposition. For Boyarin, this story constitutes "a crack in the monolith of Talmudic androcentrism, a fissure into which we can creep."[7] Beruria was an exception to the dominance of androcentrism. Hence, Boyarin sketches that on the margins of fourth-century Palestinian society, something else was happening, "something alternative to the dominant hegemonic discourse."[8] Attention to these margins allows him to historicize a past that serves as basis for remaining faithful to Talmud as well as provides grounds for change regarding women's roles within Judaism today.

In his second example, Boyarin reads across rabbinic texts attending to expressions of a particular dominant ideological position. He takes up the matter of women being urged not to speak, and in particular, not to speak of their sexual desire. Reading rabbinic texts, Boyarin demonstrates that though women's silence was the expected behavior, some texts expressing opinions on the margins quietly contest such social mores.

This leads him to consider at length a related issue involving married men. Throughout the Babylonian Talmud, men are allowed to separate themselves from their wives sexually for the purpose of total devotion to Torah study. Despite the apparent support for this practice in Talmudic texts, Boyarin shows opposing voices encoded within those same texts. Hence, he demonstrates that the Talmudic texts that ostensibly record support for this practice on behalf of men also contain evidence of strong dissension from it. With several examples he unveils the condemnation of the practice in the very stories that appear in support of married celibacy.

Further, in the midrash on Numbers 12 (Miriam's complaint against Moses,) Boyarin's close reading of this text in concert with other rabbinic materials demonstrates that Miriam's complaint was not against the wife of Moses but a complaint on her behalf. Moses himself was presumably practicing married celibacy. Boyarin reads the midrashic text then "as a form of opposition to the received tradition that Moses was a celibate husband. In order to neutralize the force of this authoritative motif, the midrash cites it and contests it at the same time by marginalizing it as the practice expected of and permitted only to Moses."[9] Thus he maintains that the midrash remains both faithful to the tradition on the practice of married celibacy for men studying Torah and, at the same time, counters it. His subsequent comparison of the Talmudic version of this tradition with the midrash further reinforces his point.

In conclusion, Boyarin surmises that on the margins of dominant hegemonic discourse there were voices and forces of resistance. He envisions both women and men who were breaking with tradition and its prescribed mold for gender behavior. It is these marginal men and women that Boyarin views as prototypes in reforming traditional Jewish gender stereotypes and practices today. Hence, he and those like him can remain rooted in the Talmudic text and tradition and still find life there. "It is this very rudimentary oppositional practice in the early culture that gives us the power now to redeem and reclaim a usable past."[10]

As a New Historicist study, Boyarin's work is particularly relevant for those working on biblical texts today. Like scholars studying the Talmudic traditions, those studying the biblical traditions have virtually no access to extraliterary documents that critics working in Renaissance studies make use of to spin their thick descriptions. Like rabbinic literature, biblical writings are of the same epistemological status. They are all literature or all documents resident within the same canon and between the same covers. Like the Talmud, there are very few materials contemporary with the biblical traditions to draw upon. However, as Boyarin both demonstrates and explains, under the assumptions of a New Historicist's view of texts, the problem virtually disappears.

> Since no assumption is made of an essential difference between literature and other texts or between textual and other practice, we read what we have as a textual practice, co-reading many different subtexts in search of access to the discourse of the society in which they were produced. We shall be engaged, then, in a kind of close-reading that aspires to be thick description at the same time.[11]

As a New Historicist study, Boyarin's reading achieves this goal and more. Charged with the working assumptions and recurring features of New Historicist kinds of studies, his investigation of the past is deeply and thoroughly tied to his own unabashed commitments and concerns in the present. And though the past he exposes is not tidy, staid, or monolithic, it is rich with transformational possibilities. For there he finds evidence of men and women who "can become for us prototypes in a reformation of traditional Jewish gender practices that nevertheless find themselves rooted firmly in the Talmudic text and tradition."[12]

HAROLD WASHINGTON ON VIOLENCE AND GENDER

In our second example of a New Historicist study, Harold Washington investigates the discursive connections between violence and gender in the

Hebrew Bible. He also considers how these constructions crisscross and rebound between the ancient and contemporary contexts and between biblical texts and the texts of scholarly interpretations. As he begins his survey of the engendering of violence, Washington does not start with a biblical tale. Rather he introduces his investigation with the 1974 story of a United States District Court Judge's attempt to overturn Lieutenant William Calley's murder conviction. Calley was a platoon leader in the Vietnam War who was convicted of leading a massacre of civilians in the village of My Lai. The circuit judge cites the prevalence of war in the Book of Joshua as the basis for the attempted exoneration of this war criminal. As it turns out, Calley was already receiving fairly lenient and even privileged treatment. Not only was Calley simply under house arrest, but he was allowed visits by girlfriends and court admirers. Though the Federal Appeals Court stayed the ruling before it could be enacted, the circuit judge's decision proved to be widely popular. The public support of Calley, particularly in the so-called Bible Belt in this country, transformed this war criminal into a hero.

Characteristic of New Historicist studies, Washington observes how cultural forces cross boundaries of time and place. He notes how the dynamic that recasts this criminal into a national hero resonates markedly with engendering of violence resident in the Hebrew Bible. In the Hebrew Bible, the "capacity for violence is synonymous with manliness, and . . . violence against feminine objects, above all, consolidates masculine identity."[13]

In the Hebrew Bible, as well as ancient Near Eastern cultures, the language of war is emblematically male. Moreover, the violence associated with warfare is closely tied to masculine sexuality. Maleness becomes aligned with victor, violence, and power. The capacity for violence becomes the measure of maleness. Hence, binary categories still operative in modern categories of gender render the female as opposite. Thus, the feminine is framed as the subjugated, plundered, defeated, and thus the powerless.

Washington notes that this connection between gender and violence is not only inscribed in, as well as constructive of, the social conditions and relations in biblical antiquity; this alignment also corroborates and reinforces the relation of violence and domination among those who claim these texts as confessional and those who critically interpret these writings. Hence, consistent with the interests of the New Historicists, he demonstrates this disquieting kinship between the production and reception of these texts.

In this connection, Washington considers the influence of German historicism and Prussian militarism on German historical critics and their reconstruction of Israel's sacral war traditions. He notes how themes such as the glorification of warfare in Israel, God as Warrior, the heroic posture of David and his male soldiers, and holy war itself are the topical preoccupations of such influential scholars as Julius Wellhausen, Friedrich Schwally, Otto Eissfeldt, and Hermann Gunkel. Historical reconstruction and interpretation of modern German biblical scholars appears glaringly related to their own cultural and political location and concerns. The dominant ethos and values related to war that are discerned in ancient Israel by this group of influential scholars appear as staggering parallels to those reigning in militaristic Germany during the era of World War I and World War II. Thus, Washington's New Historicist investigation lays bare the role our own cultural commitments play in the historical and literary outcomes of our interpretive research on the Bible.

In the second part of his study, Washington examines the Deuteronomistic law codes themselves. Though the interpretive traditions and commentaries represent and extol these laws and ordinances as protection against violence, Washington studies them for how they are, at the same time, productive of the very thing they are purported to guard against. He notes that this position in regard to law has its counterpart in the contemporary Critical Legal Studies movement. This group of legal practitioners resists assurances that law represents an objective intelligent moral order. Sharing some of the assumptions of New Historicists, this cadre of legal scholars and historians understands law as a site of contested power. Hence, they demonstrate that arguments in favor of a particular rule or ordinance can just as readily be called up in support of its opposite.

While some argue that the Deuteronomistic laws emphasize restraint and more humane treatment compared with other war codes in the ancient world, Washington discloses otherwise. He begins by observing the practical obsolescence of the Deuteronomistic war code. Still, he argues that this tradition had a profound effect on gender as an organizing category for human experience. First, the androcentric language relegates women to secondary status. Second, he demonstrates that men, by definition, are the subjects of warfare's violence while women are its victims. For example, he notes how cities and towns in the biblical tradition, the frequent object of attack in war, are framed as feminine. Even more revealing, Washington observes that the military language of attack on a city (in Hebrew) is the same language used to describe forcible seizure of a woman in a sexual assault.

Next, he demonstrates how the regulation of violence in the Deuteronomistic war code serves the interest of increasing the efficacy of exploitation more than it contributes to any humanitarian concerns. In addition, the law protects males from the exigencies of warfare itself in the instance when participation in battle jeopardizes a man's taking possession of a newly acquired wife or house or vineyard. Additionally, it fails to restrict rape in battle and it sanctions sexual coercion in the aftermath of war. Hence, Washington demonstrates that what has been often reputed as the more humane code governing war in Israel actually reinforces a kinship between gender and violence.

Maleness is associated with assaults, capture, and possession of the feminine. The female is affiliated with the conquered, the assaulted, and what is possessed in warfare as the result of these legal codes. Hence, like the arguments of the Critical Legal Studies, the Deuteronomistic war codes, though thought to protect persons against violence, are shown to do just the opposite. As discourse of male power, they deem warfare intelligible and acceptable. They can be argued as institutionalizing rape, valorizing violent acts, and thus aligning these acts as essential to male agency. In the conclusion of his study, Washington takes up how the laws governing rape, the prophetic metaphor of divine judgment as rape, and the masculinized images of women who kill in battle (such as Deborah and Jael) all contribute to and further reinforce the kinship between maleness and violence.

As a New Historicist study, Washington's article makes clear the mutually productive relationship between text and cultural identity. The violence associated with warfare and rape against a female or feminine object is shown to consolidate masculine identity. Such filiations are not innocuous discoveries about the past of those working on texts today. With New Historicist sensibility, Washington discloses the intimate connections between past and present as well as our responsibility for the social consequences of interpretations.

YVONNE SHERWOOD ON THE BOOK OF JONAH

Yvonne Sherwood investigates reading subjects as socially constrained and crafted by a complex network of economic, social, and political forces in her New Historicist study.[14] Her demonstration pursues metacommentary—

commentary on commentary—with the Book of Jonah as the focus. In her exposition of three commentaries, Sherwood challenges claims of timeless universal truths perpetuated by commentators in general. She also shows how many twentieth-century and now twenty-first century enterprises stem not from some original fourth-century B.C.E. setting (often proposed for the composition of Jonah or for the prophet), but are entangled in webs of more recent critical productions and receptions of this book. Echoes of New Historicist notions about texts resonate here—that books and stories always speak about other books and stories, as well as the cultural practices, values, and social relations at work in the production and reception of texts.

Before actually turning her attention to Jonah, Sherwood first offers her own lively expose on the contours of what she refers to as this "literary hybrid." Her brief catalogue description of recognizable features of New Historicism/Cultural Materialism has itself a New Historicist quality to it. In addition to drawing upon the contributions of now familiar names in fashioning this description (Stephen Greenblatt, H. Aram Veeser, Jeffrey N. Cox, and Larry J. Reynolds), she also draws upon the work of Eva Hoffman, author of *Lost in Translation*. Though Hoffman is not identified with these practitioners or with this movement, the reflections of this writer/journalist about her move from Poland to Canada sharply resemble features of Foucauldian histories conducted under the aegis of New Historicism. For Sherwood, this kinship suggests that the development of a New Historicism, like the histories it generates, is related to the "social forces deriving from and feeding into a wider sense of fragmentation in culture."[15]

Following her discussion of the recurring features among New Historicist kinds of projects, Sherwood turns her attention to the Book of Jonah. First, she explores commentary on the Book of Jonah in the form of sermons. In 1550, Zwinglian Protestant John Hooper delivered a series of sermons that are as much about the current social and political anxieties in England at the time as they are about Jonah. With the traumatized ship of state as the centerpiece of his reflections, Hooper rivets his attention upon the valiant soldiers who rose up and did what had to be done. They picked up that troublemaker Jonah and cast him into the sea. With his allegiance to the royal house of state, those "Jonasses" of Hooper's time included Catholic bishops, ambitious merchants, and those who disrupted the law and order of proper society. Though Sherwood makes visible the connections between the recorded sermons and the sociopolitical world of sixteenth-century England, these texts are not literal representations. "[T]exts are not windows but prisms reflecting, refracting, and even laterally inverting society's fears and ideals; and context, even for a religious sermon, must be a tangled skein of the economic, political, social and religious."[16] Here, in characteristic New Historicist fashion, she teases out the mutual fashioning going on between text and society. Hooper's words on the Bible's Word are as much being shaped by the cultural forces and anxieties of his time as they are shaping the attitudes about these same forces of his sixteenth-century environs.

The story of Jonah in Hooper's sermons not only narrates the pressing anxiety about the political and social circumstances; the mandate to throw out the dissident "Jonasses" serves as antidote to the anxieties surrounding the rise of an inexperienced King Edward, the authority of the young English Bible, and the need to keep dissenting forces in check. In the sermons, the fears of dissidence, revolt, and concerns about church authority pour into the Book of Jonah. At the same time, the sermons craft a portrait of a god-like king who with the aid of the Protestant Bible as strict disciplinarian, deals with all the "Jonasses."

In her second example, Sherwood takes up Enlightenment readings of the Book of Jonah. Here interpretations express the social desire and determination for authorizing the Bible as properly functioning within the discourse of rationalism. Within the arena of rationalistic tenets, biblical interpretation, if founded upon careful method, objective research, and sound argumentation, can actually yield the perception of the truth. At the same time the Bible is put to work in these Enlightenment interpretations addressing the social anxiety surrounding the question of the Jews and as an expression of the anti-Jewish sentiments of the period. Such social forces play themselves out in the work of scholars such as Johann David Michaelis and Johann Gottfried Eichhorn during this time. Each of these critics interprets this biblical tale as teaching that the despised heathens surpassed Jonah, the Jew, in generosity and goodness of heart. That each of these scholars working independently under the rubrics of careful method and argumentation come to the same conclusion confirmed the rationalistic platform. Jonah becomes the textual medium for addressing anxieties about Jews in the manner of rationalist intellectual debate. Even the nature of the dialogues in this story—first, between Jonah and the sailors, and then, between Jonah and God—is interpreted as authorizing the means by which rationalist schools proceed, that is, argumentation. As Sherwood's analysis of these interpretations demonstrates, these kinds of readings advance Enlightenment universalism in the guise of Christianity as superior to Jewish particularism.

In the final example, Sherwood considers an 1860 commentary on Jonah by Reverend E. D. Pusey. At this time, science and mathematics have become a part of the new discourse of power, what Sherwood calls "the ciphers of knowledge." Pusey's work itself, *The Minor Prophets, with a Commentary Explanatory and Practical,* was published one year after the appearance of Darwin's *On the Origin of the Species.* It is no coincidence then that Pusey's commentary is far more concerned with specificity, calculation, and classification of the fish than with anything having to do with Jonah. Employing Greco-Latin species labeling and algebraic calculations, Pusey makes a scientific case for the existence of the prophet-swallowing fish and even cites works of zoology to back him up. Hence, Pusey's commentary defends the Bible's authority by shrouding even a story like Jonah and the big fish with scientific credibility. In addressing the anxiety about the relevance and credibility of the Bible, he employs the language of zoology. Pusey's commentary serves to address and dismantle the doubt and even the mystery surrounding the fish. In his hands, the fish has become, like the Bible itself, a recognizable species naturalized as part of an "integral grand system of natural history."[17]

Characteristic of New Historicist concerns, Sherwood's study of these commentaries attends to the mutual fashioning going on between texts and culture. Throughout her commentary on these commentaries, she demonstrates how the Bible is employed to address concerns, desires, and anxieties of various societies and time periods. At the same time, she demonstrates how the Bible "negotiates its position in society by internalizing and transforming anxieties, and giving back to society an idealized picture of itself."[18] In addition, Sherwood, like other New Historicists interested in the discourse of power, exposes how and to what extent the voice of God blends with the voice of the dominant group. In addition, she discloses how very familiar and resonant these four-hundred-year-old readings of Jonah are for us today—particularly in regard to the status of Jews in the twentieth century, anxiety over the Bible's credibility, questions about Christianity's authority, and the showdown between universalism and particularism. Although biblical texts have a sense of "pastness," Sherwood's New Historicist work reminds us that this past is not just that of the biblical period we construct. Rather it is tightly interwoven with the cultural, geographical, religious, and political forces of the centuries of interpretation that have told and retold this story. The New Historicist assumption that texts always speak of other texts and are elaborately and intricately entwined with one another resonates again and again across this study.

6
Conclusion:
Is New Historicism
Already History?

The last chapter of an essay about a topic such as New Historicism might ordinarily be thought of as a conclusion. With the prospects of a New Historicism in biblical studies just beginning to be explored, the notion of concluding observations seems out of place. The signs of germination are only beginning to appear on the horizon. After three years as a consultation unit, a six-year group on New Historicism and the Hebrew Bible had its first year at the 2002 annual meeting of the American Academy of Religion/Society of Biblical Literature. There is already a growing collection of projects among scholars that bring a New Historicist lens to biblical texts.[1] That this series, *Guides to Biblical Scholarship*, hosts an essay exploring the promises and perils of a New Historicism in biblical studies signals further evidence of a new and growing interest. Hence, at this early stage of inquiry and investigation, any summary sounding conclusive seems premature.

Admittedly, a chapter entitled "Is New Historicism Already History?" does have an apocalyptic ring to it. It fuels expectations not so much for concluding observations but for a more disturbing discussion that "the end" is near. It suggests that the prospect for a New Historicism in biblical studies has become a fading star before it has even had a chance to be identified on the horizon. True, what some might construe as hints of "the end" seem to be cropping up in literary circles. Are they to be taken seriously or do they signal something else?

A few years ago, Stephen Moore, in his characteristically adroit, jocular manner, noted that the rise of a new movement in biblical studies often coincides with its decline or even demise in its field of origin.[2] Though he goes on to suggest that such is not the case with New Historicism, Moore's observation enkindles a concern: Is New Historicism already history? Indeed, there has been talk about the death of New Historicism in literary circles for some time.[3] However, the growing number of full-length books and journal articles under the banner of New Historicism in literary studies, as well as the health of *Representations,* the flagship journal for its first practitioners, would indicate that no one is writing an obituary just yet. However, in a recent review of Greenblatt's new book, *Hamlet in Purgatory,* Robert Alter suggests that even the *chef d'école* himself is moving away from some of his earlier practices as constitutive of this New Historicist program.[4] My own assessment of these conditions suspects that New Historicism is not so much a part of the past even in literary circles; rather it is accommodating a growing number of studies that warrant a backing away from the "Greenblattian" type of Renaissance projects of fifteen years ago. Hence, Greenblatt's own recent work, as well as that of another generation of practitioners, has become increasingly variegated and less conforming to earlier kinds of studies.

In 1997, the journal *Biblical Interpretation* devoted a whole issue to New Historicist discussions and projects conducted by biblical scholars.[5] The volume not only hosted an eclectic array of projects, practices, and interests, it also manifested wide-ranging discussions about what New Historicism is and how it might work itself out in the biblical field. No consensus emerged from the volume, but as a test drive for a New Historicism in biblical studies, the issue with all its variety and lively discussions suggested good prospects.

H. Aram Veeser, a prominent New Historicist within literary circles and editor of two readers on New Historicism, offered a concluding response to the papers.[6] Veeser's assessment of the fledgling effort, while wonderfully erudite and playful, was less than optimistic. In particular, he faulted the contributing biblical scholars for their failure to bed down with Nietzsche, or, in some instances (Sherwood's essay), to acknowledge that they had. In Veeser's assessment, New Historicism's indebtedness to Foucault should be deflected and transferred almost exclusively to Nietzsche. It is true that Nietzsche's influence on what has been called his "disconstructionist progeny"[7] can be seen in Foucault's insistence on a nontruth-oriented form of historicist study of texts. Along these lines, Foucault's contributions, in concert with those of others who have helped to craft postmodern thought, problematizes knowledge, language, and truth. This perspective is absorbed into and qualifies New Historicism's projects, and biblical scholars surely must wrestle with this. However, the uncertainty of knowledge and truth does not mandate that we jump ship with Nietzsche and abandon such quests altogether. Under the aegis of postmodernism, pursuits of knowledge or truth are not the deeds of sailors heading off into raging uncharted waters, blithely unaware of the dangers and with all lights blazing. Rather they are the objectives of those of us who knowingly move out into unknown and perhaps perilous seas. Aware of the risks and the inherent chance of failure, we take sensible precautions but are determined to persist in these pursuits. While forging ahead, we are much more mindful in our work on the biblical texts about the claims we make in regard to truth and knowledge, as well as the dangers, limitations, and social consequences involved.

Veeser levels some important challenges to the authors of these essays and to those interested in dabbling in a biblical New Historicism. He challenges us to grapple with the well-hewn practice of teleological historicizing in which biblical scholarship is entrenched. In fact, some biblical scholars working in the precincts of the history of ancient Israel are already doing just that.[8]

However, Veeser's most disqualifying arguments against this collection register under the section "a digression on method."[9] At first glance, Veeser's assessment under this heading is troubling and signals the end of a New Historicist voyage that had hardly begun in biblical studies. One might conclude that though alive and well in the literary field, New Historicism in biblical studies is already history. However, a closer assessment of Veeser's objections and comments makes me wonder if it is not Veeser's assessment that is troubled.

Veeser argues that none of the essays in this volume of *Biblical Interpretation* deserve to be ranked New Historicist because they fail "to take the risk of a frontal encounter with the social or hard sciences."[10] He goes on to earmark those essays in literary circles that he evaluates as conforming to his prescription on "method"—"persistent, intrusive assertion of one's discipline's claims within the precincts of another discipline."[11] And while none of the biblical scholars authoring these essays needs anyone to defend their work, I would argue that all of them engage materials, strategies, and theoretics from other disciplines. So the problem here, at least in Veeser's assessment, must be with their failure to be "persistent" enough or "intrusive" enough in his estimation to engage these other disciplines. In all my reading on New Historicism, Veeser's assertion here is the first I have come upon that designates a requisite methodological template for New Historicism. In fact, what characterizes New Historicists is their persistent recoil from any definitions, requirements, or prescriptions with which to designate and delimit what a New Historicist study must look like and do.[12] Moreover, the variety characterizing what they do, what they find, and how they uncover these "other histories" has become the hallmark of New Historicist studies. Hence, Veeser's methodological insistence seems unilaterally out of sync with virtually everyone else working in this terrain. In addition, I cannot help noting that Veeser's methodological requirement for induction into New Historicist ranks under his particularization of this banner would eliminate numerous authors and their essays conducted in literary circles.

As I read and reread this critic's remarks (they require several readings), his essay itself qualifies as a "site of struggle." The New Historicism that emerges from Veeser's response sounds not only characteristically "Un-New Historicist," but a lot like the property of a colonizer who demands sole and unflinching allegiance to his definition of the terrain. To number among his ranks, the biblical scholar practicing a New Historicism must employ the full complement of the "persistent and intrusive" use of the "hard sciences" as weaponry. Singular allegiance grounds his army. On this score, Veeser's unqualified rejection of Sherwood's description of New Historicism's theoretical base as "one part Derridean deconstruction, and two parts Foucauldian poststructuralism . . . and a pinch of Marx,"[13] alongside Veeser's own insistence that Nietzsche is the sole foundation here, sounded an alarm for me. Barbara Christian's characterization of this kind of rhetoric and argumentation as a "race for theory" between insiders and outsiders or against the marginalized (in this case, biblical scholars) is not only apt but, as she notes, often coincides with a colonization process well under way.[14]

Veeser's uncomely assessment makes biblical scholars "wannabe" New Historicists who might be admitted (well at least perhaps Moore and Graham) if they come up with the right material, learn his rules, and conform to Veeser's own framing of this movement. Is New Historicism already history? If it is as Veeser "represents" it—as constituting a specific taxonomy, touting uncompromising allegiance to Nietzsche with a comprehensive engagement of the "hard sciences" that would make for a new orthodoxy in literary as well as in biblical studies, then yes, New Historicism is a part of the past and passé. However, if New Historicism can be framed as discussed here—as a mind-set, characterized by recurring features, certain preoccupations, and a set of working assumptions that emancipate it from the methodological ghettoization that has so plagued the academy and at the same time that can emancipate other histories embedded in literary texts—then yes, New Historicism is charting new territory in biblical studies.

Described here as a sensibility, New Historicism motivates a reclaiming of history but with an awareness of the entanglements of the present embedded in every account of the past. Literature, as a medium for this return to the historical, is scrutinized as a site of struggle both in its production and in its reception. This rivets attention upon the diverse and contentious rather than upon the uniform and coherent within texts. In the process, New Historicism discloses and accommodates the widest variety of ways to speak about the past as well as the widest possible strategies for conducting these orations. Along these lines, New Historicism not only charts new territory but shares this space as common ground with other movements within and outside the biblical field.

Parallel movements such as feminist studies, postcolonial studies, cultural studies, and ideological investigations partake in some of New Historicism's interests and strategies, as well as approach texts with similar sets of assumptions. The influence of feminist studies in the development of a New Historicism has already been discussed in chapter two. Not only have feminists been busy documenting the case against women across all kinds of social and cultural texts well before New Historicism; we have also produced accounts of the past that have prompted others to think beyond their understanding of what they thought constituted "history." Retrieving women's voices and contributions has not only warranted their increasing visibility, but has mandated their move to a more formative position—center stage.[15]

Similarly, New Historicism and cultural studies manifest a great deal of affinities. In the first order, they are both difficult to pin down, resisting containment by any one definition. Like New Historicism, cultural studies looks at the ways that the Bible and culture mutually influence each other. Additionally, both of these programs have been fashioned upon the contributions of such thinkers as Raymond Williams and Clifford Geertz, to whom practitioners of both New Historicism and cultural studies acknowledge their debt. Among some circles in cultural studies, questions of race, ethnicity, gender, and sexuality are topics of central concern. The frequent investigation of these very topics in New Historicist projects often spin new or other histories. Moreover, the question of ideology inherent in the consideration of such topics promotes another kinship and corroboration—one between New Historicism and ideological studies. Ideological studies focus our attention on issues of power and control. New Historicists share these concerns, especially as they influence the production and reception of texts. Discourse analysis as practiced by New Historicists necessarily warrants asking questions about the ideology at work, or about what Frederic Jameson call "strategies of containment" operative in texts. Such concern with ideological factors in texts, as well as in interpretive practices, have often disclosed reigning totalizing tendencies of Euro-American reading practices. Postcolonial studies, another occupant of this common ground, lays bare these imperial influences. It challenges the context, contours, and normal procedures of biblical scholarship. In tandem with New Historicists and their interests in ideological factors, postcolonial critics scrutinize and lay bare colonial domination and power as they are embodied in biblical texts, and in their interpretations.

Beyond these currents in biblical studies, New Historicism also bears kinship ties with a British relative, "Cultural Materialism." The term "cultural materialism" came into currency in the mid 1980s when two Renaissance scholars, Jonathan Dollimore and Alan Sinfield, used it to subtitle their collection of essays, *Political Shakespeare*.[16] Early attempts to distinguish New Historicism from cultural materialism highlighted the latter's allegiance and interests as Marxist in contrast to a more eclectic array of studies and approaches among the former. In addition, New Historicists have been characterized in some circles as investigating a text in the political situation of its own day and in conversation with documents contemporary with the piece under study. By contrast, a staid textbook portrait of cultural materialism sketches a practice that studies a text in tandem with the social political situation of our own time.

Increasingly, such distinctions have faded. Practitioners in both groups work across boundaries of past and present in the materials they employ. Regularly, they trespass theoretical allegiances and host an array of strategies when approaching texts.[17] In fact, this slippage across these two currents, New Historicism and cultural materialism, is far more pronounced than any precise distinction. Sherwood's survey of these fields that prompts her to talk about New Historicism as the "hybrid" New Historicism/cultural materialism is apt.[18]

Given New Historicism's resemblance to cultural materialism, in tandem with its shared interests, assumptions, and strategies with these other currents in biblical studies, as well as its persistent boundary-crossing into other disciplines, it is fair to wonder what makes New Historicism what it is. Does this literary program's kinship to other practices and paradigms, along with its accommodation of such a variety of inquiry, explain our inability to serve up this entrée with a more precise recipe?

Resisting the fracturing that has so characterized the biblical field, New Historicism refuses identification and explication as method. Understanding the complexity of the past, New Historicism resists any historicizing of itself that would tie it solely to any one theoretical base or align it with a single founding figure and his or her work. Aside from a fairly fluid litany of recurring features, New Historicism provides no creed for its practitioners to avow. And as those working within Renaissance studies would readily affirm, New Historicism's overarching feature is its resistance to definition.

Is New Historicism a mirage? Or is it, in all its variety and nonspecificity, a refreshing and optimistic commentary about a growing shift both in the academy and in biblical studies—a shift away from the splintering of methodological specialization that has so characterized the field over the past century? New Historicism readily shares concerns and features with other taxonomies (Third World studies, African American studies, feminist studies, postcolonial studies, and so on). And while it practices a kind of discourse analysis of literature bent on emancipating voices, highlighting overlooked people and practices, and producing other histories, it seems not to expend much discussion distinguishing itself from these other movements.

No, New Historicism is no mirage. Rather the appeal for a New Historicism in biblical studies at this time is symptomatic of another condition. Biblical studies is itself becoming a montage with New Historicism as part of the display. Across this postmodern manifestation of interpretive practices, a growing number of critics have become less interested in distinguishing and defending what they do from the work of other critics. Abandoning the

75

high degree of specialization, they are more interested in crossing method-ological and disciplinary borders. And while their participation in this mar-ket of exchange results in an ever-increasing number of lenses with which to read and interpret the biblical text, they find themselves united not so much by a sameness in their outcomes or methods as by a growing consensus about what they are up to.

Increasingly, critics working on the biblical texts have begun to recognize and claim the political import of what they do when they interpret texts. They understand that there are social consequences tied to the outcome of their work. Hence, a commitment to work in biblical studies increasingly enjoins a commitment to social change on the part of those who would par-ticipate in this practice. Given the recognized influence of the Bible on cul-ture in the past and in the present, a cadre of critics (whether practitioners of New Historicism, postcolonial studies, feminist studies, cultural studies, and so on) determined to be equally influential on the future by virtue of what they do with these texts in the present is not a bad prospect for the next era in biblical studies.

Abbreviations

BCSR	*Bulletin for the Council on the Study of Religion*
BibInt	*Biblical Interpretation*
CAnth	*Current Anthropology*
CSSH	*Comparative Studies in Society and History*
CulCrit	*Culture Critique*
ELH	*English Literary History*
ELR	*English Literary Renaissance*
GBS	*Guides to Biblical Scholarship*
HTR	*Harvard Theological Review*
IDB	*Interpreter's Dictionary of the Bible*
JBL	*Journal of Biblical Literature*
JFSR	*Journal of Feminist Studies in Religion*
JR	*Journal of Religion*
JSOT	*Journal for the Study of the Old Testament*
JSOTSup	JSOT Supplement Series
MLQ	*Modern Language Quarterly*
PMLA	*Proceedings of the Modern Language Association*
SAQ	*South Atlantic Quarterly*
TLS	*The Times Literary Supplement* (London)

Notes

1. Introduction

1. Over twenty years ago, Paul Achtemeier and Gene Tucker were already remarking that an influx of new methods was the most characteristic feature of biblical studies. See Paul J. Achtemeier and Gene M. Tucker, "Biblical Studies: The State of the Discipline," *BCSR* 3 (June 1980): 73–74.

2. The expression "setting in life" is used here for Hermann Gunkel's phrase *Sitz im Leben*. As the pioneer of form criticism, Gunkel used this phrase to refer to the situation which produced and maintained a particular genre. See Gunkel, "Israelite Literary History," in *Water for a Thirsty Land: Israelite Literature and Religion*, edited by K. C. Hanson, Fortress Classics in Biblical Studies (Minneapolis: Fortress Press, 2001) 35–36.

3. Mark Allan Powell, *The Bible and Modern Literary Criticism: A Critical Assessment and Annotated Bibliography* (New York: Greenwood, 1992).

4. Stephen Greenblatt, *Learning To Curse—Essays in Early Modern Culture* (New York: Routledge, 1990) 3.

5. Louis Montrose, "Renaissance Literary Studies and the Subject of History," *ELR* 16 (winter 1986): 6.

6. Joel Fineman, "The History of the Anecdote: Fiction and Fiction," in *The New Historicism*, ed. H. Aram Veeser (New York: Routledge, 1989) 52.

7. Catherine Gallagher, "Marxism and the New Historicism," in Veeser, ed., *The New Historicism*, 37.

8. Montrose, 6.

9. Fineman, 52.

10. See Gina Hens-Piazza, *Of Methods, Monarchs, and Meanings—An Approach to Sociorhetorical Interpretation* (Macon, Ga.: Mercer Univ. Press, 1996).

11. Fineman, 57.

12. Michael McCanles, "The Authentic Discourse of the Renaissance," *Diacritics* 10 (1980): 85.

13. Stephen Greenblatt, "Introduction" in *Forms of Power and the Power of Forms*, ed. Stephen Greenblatt (Norman, Okla.: Pilgrim, 1982) 3–6.

14. Stephen Greenblatt, *Renaissance Self-Fashioning* (Chicago: Univ. of Chicago Press, 1980) 5.

15. These labels have been set forth, respectively, in Herbert Lindenberger, "Toward (and After) a New History in Literary Study," in *The History in Literature: On Value, Genre, Institutions* (New York: Columbia Univ. Press, 1990) 189–210; Robert Weimann, "Towards a Literary Theory of Ideology: Mimesis, Representation, Authority," in *Shakespeare Reproduced: The Text in History and Ideology*, ed. Jean E. Howard and Marion F. O'Connor (New York: Methuen, 1987) 265–72; and Howard Horitz, "I Can't Remember: Skepticism, Synthetic Histories, Critical Action," *SAQ* 87 (fall 1988): 787–820.

16. Lee Patterson, "Introduction: Critical Historicism and Medieval Studies," in *Literary Practice and Social Change in Britain, 1380–1530*, ed. Lee Patterson (Berkeley: Univ. of California Press, 1990) 1.

17. Daniel Boyarin, "Rabbinic Resistance to Male Domination: A Case Study in Talmudic Cultural Poetics," in *Interpreting Judaism in a Postmodern Age*, ed. Steven Kepnes (New York: New York Univ. Press, 1996) 118–41.

18. Cultural materialism is the British counterpart of New Historicism. Ten years ago, efforts were made to carefully distinguish cultural materialism from the New Historicism current in American universities. Today, these distinctions are less clear. See the concluding chapter for further discussion.

2. Historicizing the New Historicism

1. Edward Pechter, "The New Historicism and Its Discontents: Politicizing Renaissance Drama," *PMLA* 102 (May 1987): 292.

2. For a discussion of Marxist tradition as it influences New Historicism, see Pierre Machery, *A Theory of Literary Production*, trans. Geoffrey

Wall (London: Routledge and Kegan Paul, 1978); Louis Althusser, "Ideological State Apparatuses," in *Lenin and Philosophy and Other Essays*, trans. Ben Brewster (New York: Monthly Review Press, 1971) 123–73; and Terry Eagleton, *Criticism and Ideology: A Study in Marxist Literary Theory* (London: New Left Books, 1976).

3. Catherine Gallagher and Stephen Greenblatt, *Practicing New Historicism* (Chicago: Univ. of Chicago Press, 2000) 9.

4. Robert Hodge, *Literature as Discourse: Textual Strategies in English and History* (Baltimore: Johns Hopkins Univ. Press, 1990) viii.

5. For a clear exposition of Foucault's work, see Alan Sheridan, *Michel Foucault: The Will to Truth* (London: Tavistock, 1980).

6. For an overview of Foucault's contribution to historical study, see Mark Poster, "The Future According to Foucault: The Archaeology of Knowledge and Intellectual History," in *Modern European Intellectual History: Reappraisals and New Perspectives*, ed. Dominick LaCapra and Steven L. Kaplan (Ithaca: Cornell Univ. Press, 1982) 111–52.

7. Hayden White, "Michael Foucault," in *Structuralism and Since*, ed. J. Sturrock (Oxford: Oxford Univ. Press, 1979) 93.

8. Michel Foucault, *Power/Knowledge: Selected Interviews and Other Writings 1972–1977*, ed. Colin Gordon (New York: Pantheon, 1980) 119.

9. The influence of these groups is pointed out by Carolyn Porter in "Are We Being Historical Yet?" *SAQ* 87 (1988): 743–86. For a discussion of feminist influence on the development of New Historicism, see Judith Newton, "History as Usual? Feminism and the 'New Historicism,'" *CulCrit* 9 (spring 1988): 87–121; and Judith Todd, *Feminist Literary History* (New York: Routledge, 1988) 98–99.

10. Gallagher and Greenblatt, *Practicing*, 11.

11. Newton, "History as Usual?" 99.

12. Clifford Geertz, "Thick Description: Toward an Interpretive Theory of Culture," in *The Interpretation of Cultures* (New York: Basic Books, 1973) 3–30. The expression "thick description" was first used by Gilbert Ryle in his essays on thinking. Compare Gilbert Ryle, "Thinking and Reflecting" and "The Thinking of Thoughts: What Is 'Le Penseur' Doing?" in *Collected Papers*, vol. 2 of *Collected Essays, 1929–1968* (London: Hutchinson, 1971) 465–96.

13. Geertz, "Thick Description," 9.

14. Louis Montrose, "A Poetics of Renaissance Culture," *Criticism* 23 (1981): 357.

15. Roger Kessing, "Anthropology as Interpretive Quest," *CAnth* 28 (1987): 116.

16. Raymond Williams, *Marxism and Literature* (Oxford: Oxford Univ. Press, 1978).

17. Ibid., 112.

18. Ibid., 112.

19. Hayden White, *Tropics of Discourse: Essays in Cultural Criticism* (Baltimore: Johns Hopkins Univ. Press, 1978).

20. Bakhtin's work on *heteroglossia* can be found in *The Dialogic Imagination: Four Essays*, ed. Michael Holquist, trans. Caryl Emerson and Michael Holquist (Austin: Univ. of Texas Press, 1981) 259–422.

21. Edward W. Said, *Orientalism* (New York: Random House, 1978).

22. Frank Lentricchia, *After the New Criticism* (Chicago: Univ. of Chicago Press, 1980) xii–xiv.

23. Ibid., xiv.

24. Stephen Greenblatt, *Renaissance Self-Fashioning* (Chicago: Univ. of Chicago Press, 1980).

25. Stephen Greenblatt, *Shakespearean Negotiations: The Circulation of Social Energy in Renaissance England* (Berkeley: Univ. of California Press, 1988); *Learning to Curse: Essays in Early Modern Culture* (New York: Routledge, 1990); *Marvelous Possessions: The wonder of the New World* (Chicago: Univ. of Chicago Press, 1991); *Hamlet in Purgatory* (Princeton: Princeton Univ. Press, 2001).

26. Jerome McGann, *The Romantic Ideology: A Critical Investigation* (Chicago: Univ. of Chicago Press, 1983).

27. Sacvan Bercovitch and Myra Jehlen, eds., *Ideology and Classic American Literature* (Cambridge: Cambridge Univ. Press, 1986).

28. Louis Montrose, "Renaissance Literary Studies and the Subject of History," *ELR* 16 (winter 1986): 11.

29. Ibid.

30. Gregory S. Jay, *America the Scrivener: Deconstruction and the Subject of Literary History* (Ithaca: Cornell Univ. Press, 1990) 236–54.

31. Jerome McGann, *Social Values and Poetic Acts: The Historical Judgment of Literary Work* (Cambridge: Harvard Univ. Press, 1988) 1–10, 95–131.

32. For example, in Walter Wink, *The Bible in Human Transformation*

(Philadelphia: Fortress Press, 1973) 7–8, the author declares historical criticism bankrupt.

33. For example, Robert Culley conducts a narrative analysis and David Jobling conducts a structural analysis on the texts in Genesis 2–3. See Culley, "Action Sequences in Genesis 2–3," in *SBL Seminar Papers*, vol. 1, ed. Paul J. Achtemeier (Missoula, Mont.: Scholars, 1978) 51–59 and Jobling, "A Structural Analysis of Genesis 2.4b—3.24," *SBL Seminar Papers*, vol. 1, ed. Paul J. Achtemeier (Missoula, Mont.: Scholars, 1978) 61–69. By contrast, Phyllis Bird and Carol Meyers study the various contexts of the Genesis stories and how these contexts inform interpretation. See Bird, "Male and Female He Created Them: Gen. 1.27b in the Context of the Priestly Account of Creation," *HTR* 77 (1981): 129–59, and Meyers, "Gender Roles and Genesis 3.16 Revisited," in *The Word of the Lord Shall God Forth*, ed. Carol Meyers and Marion F. O'Connor (Philadelphia: American Schools of Oriental Research, 1983) 337–54.

34. For a discussion of the incompatibility of literary and historical paradigms, see Hans Frei, *The Eclipse of the Biblical Narrative* (New Haven: Yale Univ. Press, 1974) 150–54.

35. Brevard S. Childs argues for the determinacy of the canonical meaning. See Childs, *Introduction to the Old Testament as Scripture* (Philadelphia: Fortress Press, 1979) 74–75. James Barr criticizes Childs's discussion. See Barr, *Holy Scripture* (Philadelphia: Westminster, 1983) 145 and 154. Influenced by Derrida, David Jobling and Mieka Bal argue for the indeterminacy of texts' meaning. See Jobling, *The Sense of the Biblical Narrative—Structural Analyses in the Hebrew Bible II*, JSOTSup 39 (Sheffield: JSOT Press, 1986) 12–13, and Bal, *Lethal Love—Feminist Literary Readings of Biblical Love Stories* (Bloomington: Indiana Univ. Press, 1987) 13–14. In addition, two volumes of *Semeia* have been devoted to this very debate; Robert Culley and Robert B. Robinson, eds., *Semeia*, vol. 62 (1993) and vol. 71 (1995).

3. On the Differences between Historicism and the New Historicism

1. Throughout this chapter, I use the terms *historicism* and *historicists* to refer to conventional historicist practices and practitioners (what some might call an "old" historicism) in contrast to New Historicism and the New Historicists.

2. Frederic Jameson, *The Political Unconscious: Narrative as a Socially Symbolic Act* (Ithaca: Cornell Univ. Press, 1981).

3. R. G. Collingwood, *The Idea of History* (Oxford: Oxford Univ. Press, 1956) 9–10.

4. For a recent rehearsal of the problem and its history, see Walter Brueggemann, *Theology of the Old Testament: Testimony, Dispute, Advocacy* (Minneapolis: Fortress Press, 1997) 9–10.

5. Krister Stendahl, "Biblical Theology, Contemporary," in *IDB* 1, 418–32.

6. Stephen Greenblatt, *Learning to Curse: Essays in Early Modern Culture* (New York: Routledge, 1990) 167.

7. Ibid.

8. Louis Montrose, "New Historicisms," in *Redrawing the Boundaries,* ed. Stephen Greenblatt and G. Gunn (New York: MLA, 1992) 392–418.

9. Jeffrey N. Cox and Larry J. Reynolds, introduction to *New Historical Literary Study,* eds. Cox and Reynolds (Princeton: Princeton Univ. Press, 1993) 4.

10. Jean Howard, "The New Historicism in Renaissance Studies," *ELR* 16 (winter 1986): 21.

11. In addition, Carroll footnotes some of the more recent of these works. Compare Robert Carroll, "Clio and Canons," *BibInt* 5 (1997): 306–7.

12. See "Bible and the Cultural Collective," in *The Postmodern Bible* (New Haven, Connecticut: Yale Univ. Press, 1995) and A. K. M. Adam, *What Is Postmodern Biblical Criticism?* GBS (Minneapolis: Fortress Press, 1995) for recent currents in postmodern biblical interpretation.

13. Fred Burnett, "Postmodern Biblical Exegesis: The Eve of Historical Criticism," *Semeia* 51 (1990): 51.

14. The collapse of these distinctions under a New Historicism is discussed in the chapter on characteristics of New Historicism.

15. Peter Barry, *Beginning Theory: An Introduction to Literary and Cultural Theory* (Manchester: Manchester Univ. Press, 1995) 175.

16. Martin Noth, *Überlieferungsgeschichtliche Studien* (Tübingen: Niemeyer, 1957).

17. Norman Gottwald, "Social Class and Ideology in Isaiah 40–55: An Eagletonian Reading," *Semeia* 59 (1992): 43–57.

18. See Brook Thomas's discussion, "The New Historicism and Other Old-Fashioned Topics," in *The New Historicism,* ed. H. Aram Veeser (London: Routledge, 1989) 182–203.

19. This relationship between past and present as fundamental to the New Historicist project is developed in Louis Montrose, "Renaissance Literary Studies and the Subject of History," *ELR* 16 (1986): 7–8. It will be discussed in more detail in the chapter on "Recognizable Features."

20. Brian Rosenberg, "Historicizing the New Historicism: Understanding the Past in Criticism and Fiction," *MLQ* 50 (1989): 376.

21. Frank Lentricchia, *After the New Criticism* (Chicago: Univ. of Chicago Press, 1980) xii–xiv. See *The New Historicism*, ed. Veeser, 20.

22. Jerome McGann, *The Beauty of Inflections: Literary Investigations in Historical Method and Theory* (Oxford: Clarendon Press, 1985) 10.

23. Louis Montrose, "Renaissance Literary Studies and the Subject of History," *ELR* 16 (winter 86): 8.

24. Jeremy Hawthorn, *Cunning Passages* (London: Arnold Press, 1996) 56.

25. Hayden White, *Tropics of Discourse: Essays in Cultural Criticism* (Baltimore: Johns Hopkins Univ. Press, 1985) 58, italics in original.

4. Recurring Characteristics of New Historicist Studies

1. Gene M. Tucker, *Form Criticism of the Old Testament*, GBS (Philadelphia: Fortress Press, 1971) 10–16.

2. Norman Habel, *Literary Criticism of the Old Testament*, GBS (Philadelphia: Fortress Press, 1971) 6–7.

3. Walter E. Rast, *Tradition History and the Old Testament*, GBS (Philadelphia: Fortress Press, 1972) 19–32.

4. Edgar Krentz, *The Historical-Critical Method*, GBS (Philadelphia: Fortress Press, 1975) 41–54.

5. Mark Allan Powell, *What Is Narrative Criticism?* GBS (Minneapolis: Fortress Press, 1990).

6. John Barton, *Reading the Old Testament* (Louisville: Westminster John Knox, 1996) 244.

7. H. Aram Veeser, *The New Historicist Reader* (New York: Routledge, 1994).

8. Ibid., 5.

9. Susan Lochrie Graham and Stephen D. Moore, "The Quest of the New Historicist Jesus," *BibInt* 5 (1997): 438–64.

10. Julia Kristeva, *Semeiotike: Recherches pour une Semanalysis* (Paris: Seuil, 1969) 146.

11. In *Shakespearean Negotiations: The Circulation of Social Energy in Renaissance England* (Berkeley: Univ. of California Press, 1988) 2–4, Stephen Greenblatt discusses his own uneasiness with the monolithic constructions that once dominated his work. His study of Renaissance self-fashioning had begun to persuade him that "Elizabethan and Jacobean visions of hidden unity seemed like anxious rhetorical attempts to conceal cracks, conflict and disarray" (2).

12. Brian Rosenberg, "Historicizing the New Historicism: Understanding the Past in Criticism and Fiction," *MLQ* 50 (1989): 376.

13. Lori L. Rowlett, *Joshua and the Rhetoric of Violence: A New Historicist Analysis,* JSOTSup 226 (Sheffield: Sheffield Academic Press, 1996) 29.

14. Stephen Greenblatt, *Renaissance Self-Fashioning* (Chicago: Univ. of Chicago Press, 1980) 5.

15. Maaike Meijer, "Countering Textual Violence—On the Critique of Representation and the Importance of Teaching Its Methods," *Women's Studies International Forum* 16 (1993): 367–78.

16. Edward Said, *Orientalism* (New York: Vantage, 1978).

17. Stephen Greenblatt, "Reading National Geographic," *The New Yorker* (October 11, 1993) 112.

18. Ibid.

19. Ibid.

20. See Gina Hens-Piazza, "Forms of Violence and the Violence of Forms: Two Cannibal Mothers before a King (2 Kgs 6:24-33)," *JFSR* 14.1 (1998): 91–104.

21. Brook Thomas, *New Historicism and Other Old-Fashioned Topics* (Princeton: Princeton Univ. Press, 1991).

22. Stanley Fish, "Commentary: The Young and the Restless," in *The New Historicism,* ed. H. Aram Veeser (New York: Routledge, 1989) 303–16.

23. J. McGann, "The Third World of Criticism," in M. Levinson et al., eds., *Rethinking Historicism* (Oxford: Blackwell, 1989).

24. Daniel Boyarin, "Rabbinic Resistance to Male Domination: A Case Study in Talmudic Cultural Poetics," in *Interpreting Judaism in a Postmodern Age,* ed. Steven Kepnes (New York: New York Univ. Press, 1996) 118–41.

25. Alan Liu, "The Power of Formalism: The New Historicism," *ELH* 56 (1989): 753.

26. Harold Washington, "Violence and the Construction of Gender in the Hebrew Bible: A New Historicist Approach," *BibInt* 5 (1997): 324–63.

27. Stephen Moore and Janice Capel Anderson, "Taking It Like a Man: Masculinity in 4 Maccabees," *JBL* 117 (1998): 249–72.

28. Umberto Eco, *Postscript to the Name of the Rose*, trans. William Weaver (San Diego: Jovanovich, 1983) 20.

29. Ellen van Wolde, "From Text via Text to Meaning: Intertextuality and Its Implications," in *Words Become Worlds: Semantic Studies of Genesis 1–11*, *BibInt* 6 (1994): 163.

30. Michel Foucault, *The Archaeology of Knowledge*, trans. A. M. Sheridan Smith (London: Tavistock, 1972) 45.

31. Peter Barry, *Beginning Theory—An Introduction to Literary and Cultural Theory* (Manchester: Manchester Univ. Press, 1995) 172.

32. Greenblatt, *Shakespearean Negotiations*, 86.

33. Hugh O'Grady, *The Modernist Shakespeare* (Oxford Univ. Press, 1991) 226.

34. Richard Wilson and Richard Dutton, eds., *New Historicism and Renaissance Drama* (London: Longman, 1992) 8, italics in original.

35. Dominick LaCapra, *Soundings in Critical Theory* (Ithaca: Cornell Univ. Press, 1989) 193.

36. Toril Moi, ed., *The Kristeva Reader* (New York: Columbia Univ. Press, 1986) 35–61.

37. Stephen Greenblatt, "Resonance and Wonder," in *Learning to Curse* (London: Routledge, 1990) 170.

38. Van Wolde, "From Text via Text," 160–200.

39. Yvonne Sherwood, "Rocking the Boat: Jonah and the New Historicism," *BibInt* 5 (1997): 364–403.

40. Ibid., 377.

41. Van Wolde, "From Text via Text," 163.

42. Frederic Jameson, *The Political Unconscious: Narrative as a Socially Symbolic Act* (Ithaca, N.Y.: Cornell Univ. Press, 1981) 52–53.

5. New Historicism—Three Illustrations

1. Daniel Boyarin, "Rabbinic Resistance to Male Domination: A Case Study in Talmudic Cultural Poetics," in *Interpreting Judaism in a Postmodern*

Age, ed. Steven Kepnes (New York: New York Univ. Press, 1996) 11–141.

2. Harold Washington, "Violence and the Construction of Gender in the Hebrew Bible: A New Historicist Approach," *BibInt* 5 (1997): 324–63.

3. Yvonne Sherwood, "Rocking the Boat: Jonah and the New Historicism," *BibInt* 5 (1997): 364–403.

4. Part of this essay first appeared as Boyarin's contribution to the series in *Carnal Israel: Reading Sex in Talmudic Culture,* The New Historicism: Studies in Cultural Poetics 25 (Berkeley: Univ. of California Press, 1993) 181–82.

5. Boyarin is here describing discourse in the Foucauldian sense as cited in Robert Hodge, *Literature as Discourse: Textual Strategies in English and History,* Parallax (Baltimore: Johns Hopkins Univ. Press, 1990) 121.

6. Boyarin, "Rabbinic Resistance," 125.

7. Ibid., 126.

8. Ibid., 136.

9. Ibid., 134.

10. Ibid., 137.

11. Ibid., 123.

12. Ibid., 136.

13. Washington, "Violence and the Construction of Gender," 326.

14. For an expanded study of this text, along with an accompanying discussion on New Historicism, see Yvonne Sherwood, *A Biblical Text and Its Afterlives: The Survival of Jonah in Western Culture* (Cambridge: Cambridge Univ. Press, 2000).

15. Sherwood, "Rocking the Boat," 367.

16. Ibid., 382.

17. Ibid., 398.

18. Ibid.

6. Conclusion: Is New Historicism Already History?

1. For example, Mary Ann Tolbert, "The Gospel in Greco-Roman Culture," in *The Book and the Text: The Bible and Literary Theory,* ed. Regina M. Schwartz (Oxford: Basil Blackwell, 1990) 258–74; Lori Rowlett, "Inclusion, Exclusion and Marginality in the Book of Joshua," *JSOT* 55 (1992): 15–23; idem, *Joshua and the Rhetoric of Violence: A New Historicist Analysis,* JSOT-Sup 226 (Sheffield: Sheffield Academic, 1996); Gina Hens-Piazza, "Forms of

Violence and the Violence of Forms: Two Cannibal Mothers before a King (2 Kgs 6:24-33)," *JFSR* 14.1 (1998): 91–104; Stephen Moore, ed., a thematic issue of *BibInt* 5 (1997) entitled "A New Historicism"; Stephen Moore and Janice Capel Anderson, "Taking It Like a Man: Masculinity in 4 Maccabees," *JBL* 117 (1998): 249–72; Yvonne Sherwood, *A Biblical Text and Its Afterlives: The Survival of Jonah in Western Culture* (Cambridge: Cambridge Univ. Press, 2000. In addition, New Historicism also is receiving attention by those tracking future directions for literary studies of the Bible. See, for example, John R. Donahue, "The Literary Turn and New Testament Theology: Detour or New Direction?" *JR* 76 (1996): 250–75; and A. K. M. Adams, *What Is Postmodern Biblical Criticism?* GBS (Minneapolis: Fortress Press, 1995) 45–48, 57–58.

2. Stephen Moore, "History after Theory? Biblical Studies and the New Historicism," *BibInt* 5 (1997) 289–90.

3. As early as 1991, Terry Eagleton, in his essay "The Historian as Body Snatcher" (*TLS* 18 [January 1991]: 7) was already forecasting the demise of New Historicism.

4. Robert Alter, "Just Passing Through," review of *Hamlet in Purgatory,* by Stephen Greenblatt, *New York Times* (May 20, 2001) sec. 7, p. 45.

5. Stephen Moore, ed., "A New Historicism," *BibInt* 5 (1997).

6. H. Aram Veeser, "Christianity, Wild Turkey, and Syphilis," *BibInt* 5 (1997) 465–81. See also *The New Historicism* (New York: Routledge, 1989) and *The New Historicism Reader* (New York: Routledge, 1994), both edited by Veeser.

7. Frank Lentricchia, "Foucault's Legacy," in *The New Historicism,* 241.

8. See, for example, Philip R. Davies, *In Search of "Ancient Israel,"* JSOTSup 148 (Sheffield: JSOT Press, 1992) or Keith W. Whitelam, *The Invention of Ancient Israel—The Silencing of Palestinian History* (London: Routledge, 1996).

9. Veeser, "Christianity, Wild Turkey, and Syphilis," 469.

10. Ibid.

11. Ibid., 470–71.

12. In "Towards a Poetics of Culture," in *The New Historicism,* 1–2, one of the earlier attempts to set out what New Historicism is and how it does what it does, Greenblatt asserts that New Historicism is "no doctrine" and certainly not "a single critical practice."

13. Yvonne Sherwood, "Rocking the Boat: Jonah and the New Historicism," *BibInt* 5 (1997): 367.

14. Barbara Christian, "The Race for Theory," *Cultural Critique* 6 (spring 1987): 55.

15. However, Judith Newton ("History as Usual? Feminism and the New Historicism," *CulCrit* 9 [spring 1988]: 92) reminds us that speaking from the margins has its advantages and uses, too.

16. Jonathon Dollimore, and Alan Sinfield, eds., *Political Shakespeare: New Essays in Cultural Materialism,* 2nd ed. (Manchester: Manchester Univ. Press, 1994).

17. See John Brannigan, *New Historicism and Cultural Materialism: Transitions* (New York: St. Martin's, 1998).

18. Sherwood, "Rocking the Boat," 366.

For Further Reading

Discussions and Collections of Representative Essays within Literary Circles

Brannigan, John. *New Historicism and Cultural Materialism: Transitions.* New York: St. Martin's Press, 1998.

Cadzow, Hunter. "New Historicism." In *Johns Hopkins Guide to Literary Theory and Criticism,* 534–40. Baltimore: Johns Hopkins Univ. Press.

Coates, Christopher. "What Was the New Historicism?" *The Centennial Review* 37 (spring 1993): 267–80.

Colebrook, Claire. *New Literary Histories: New Historicism and Contemporary Criticism.* Manchester: Manchester Univ. Press, 1997.

Cox, Jeffrey N., and Larry J. Reynolds, eds. *New Historical Literary Study: Essays on Reproducing Texts, Representing History.* Princeton: Princeton Univ. Press, 1993.

Cox, John D. "New Historicism." In *Contemporary Literary Theory: A Christian Appraisal,* ed. Clarence Walhout and Leland Ryken, 252–70. Grand Rapids: Eerdmans, 1991.

Dollimore, Jonathon. "Introduction: Shakespeare, Cultural Materialism and the New Historicism." In *Political Shakespeare: New Essays in Cultural Materialism,* 2–17. Ithaca, N.Y.: Cornell Univ. Press, 1985.

Dollimore, Jonathon, and Alan Sinfield, eds. *Political Shakespeare: New Essays in Cultural Materialism.* 2nd ed. Manchester: Manchester Univ. Press, 1994.

Fineman, Joel. "The History of the Anecdote: Fiction and Fiction." In *The New Historicism,* ed. H. Aram Veeser, 49–76. New York: Routledge, 1989.

Gallagher, Catherine. *The Industrial Revolution of English Fiction: Social Discourse and Narrative Form.* Chicago: Univ. of Chicago Press, 1988.

Gallagher, Catherine, and Stephen Greenblatt. *Practicing New Historicism.* Chicago: Univ. of Chicago Press, 2000.

Greenblatt, Stephen. *Hamlet in Purgatory.* Princeton: Princeton Univ. Press, 2001.

———. *Marvelous Possessions: The Wonder of the New World.* Chicago: Univ. of Chicago Press, 1991.

———. *Learning To Curse: Essays in Early Modern Culture.* New York: Routledge, 1990.

———. *Shakespearean Negotiations: The Circulation of Social Energy in Renaissance England.* Berkeley: Univ. of California Press, 1988.

———. "The Forms of Power and the Power of Forms in the Renaissance." *Genre* 15 (1982): 1–4.

———. *Renaissance Self-Fashioning: From More to Shakespeare.* Chicago: Univ. of Chicago Press, 1980.

Hamilton, Paul. *Historicism: The New Critical Idiom.* London: Routledge, 1996.

Hart, Jonathon. "New Historicism: Taking History into Account." *Ariel* 22 (January 1991): 93–107.

Hawthorn, Jeremy. *Cunning Passages: New Historicism, Cultural Materialism, and Marxism in the Contemporary Literary Debate.* London: Arnold Press, 1996.

Howard, Jean. "The New Historicism in Renaissance Studies." *ELR* 16 (winter 1986): 13–43.

Jay, Gregory. "Ideology and the New Historicism." *Arizona Quarterly* 49 (spring 1993): 141–56.

Lehan, Richard. "The Theoretical Limits of the New Historicism." *New Literary History* 21 (spring 1990): 533–53.

Montrose, Louis. "Renaissance Literary Studies and the Subject of History." *ELR* 16 (winter 1986): 5–12.

———. "New Historicisms." In *Redrawing the Boundaries: The Transformation of English and American Literary Studies,* ed. Stephen Greenblatt and Giles Gunn, 392–418. New York: MLA, 1992.

Morris, Wesley. *Toward a New Historicism.* Princeton: Princeton Univ. Press, 1972.

Newton, Judith. "History as Usual? Feminism and the New Historicism." *CulCrit* 9 (spring 1988): 87–121.

Rosenberg, Brian. "Historicizing the New Historicism: Understanding the Past in Criticism and Fiction." *MLQ* 50 (1989): 375–92.

Sinfield, Alan. *Faultlines: Cultural Materialism and the Politics of Dissident Reading.* Oxford: Clarendon, 1992.

Stempel, Daniel. "History and Postmodern Literary Theory." In *Tracing Literary Theory,* ed. Joseph Natoli, 80–104. Urbana: Univ. of Illinois Press, 1987.

Thomas, Brook. *New Historicism and Other Old-Fashioned Topics.* Princeton: Princeton Univ. Press, 1991.

Veeser, H. Aram. *The New Historicist Reader.* New York: Routledge, 1994.

Wilson, Richard, and Richard Dutton, eds. *New Historicism and Renaissance Drama.* London: Longman, 1992.

Winn, James A. "An Old Historian Looks at the New Historicism." *CSSH* 35 (1993): 859–71.

Discussions and Representative Essays of New Historicism within Biblical Studies

Adams, A. K. M. *What Is Postmodern Biblical Criticism?* GBS. Minneapolis: Fortress Press, 1995.

Boyarin, Daniel. *Carnal Israel: Reading Sex in Talmudic Culture.* The New Historicism: Studies in Cultural Poetics 25. Berkeley, California: Univ. of California Press, 1993.

Carroll, Robert. "Clio and Canons." *BibInt* 5 (1997): 306–7.

Donahue, John R. "The Literary Turn and New Testament Theology: Detour or New Direction?" *JR* 76 (1996): 250–75.

Hens-Piazza, Gina. "Forms of Violence and the Violence of Forms: Two Cannibal Mothers before a King (2 Kgs 6:24-33)." *JFSR* 14.1 (1998): 91–104.

Lochrie Graham, Susan, and Stephen D. Moore. "The Quest of the New Historicist Jesus." *BibInt* 5 (1997): 438–64.

Marsh, Clive. "Quests of the Historical Jesus in New Historicist Perspective." *BibInt* 5 (1997): 403–37.

Moore, Stephen D. "History after Theory? Biblical Studies and the New Historicism." *BibInt* 5 (1997): 289–99.

Moore, Stephen D., ed. New Historicism issue. *BibInt* 5. Leiden: Brill, 1997.

Moore, Stephen, and Janice Capel Anderson. "Taking It Like a Man: Masculinity in 4 Maccabees." *JBL* 117 (1998): 249–72.

Rowlett, Lori L. *Joshua and the Rhetoric of Violence: A New Historicist Analysis,* JSOTSup 226. Sheffield: Sheffield Academic Press, 1996.

———. "Inclusion, Exclusion and Marginality in the Book of Joshua." *JSOT* 55 (1992): 15–23.

Sherwood, Yvonne. *A Biblical Text and Its Afterlives: The Survival of Jonah in Western Culture.* Cambridge: Cambridge Univ. Press, 2000.

———. "Rocking the Boat: Jonah and the New Historicism." *BibInt* 5 (1997): 364–403.

Tolbert, Mary Ann. "The Gospel in Greco-Roman Culture." In *The Book and the Text: The Bible and Literary Theory,* ed. Regina M. Schwartz, 258–74. Oxford: Blackwell, 1990.

Washington, Harold. "Violence and the Construction of Gender in the Hebrew Bible: A New Historicist Approach." *BibInt* 5 (1997): 324–63.